Vegetarian

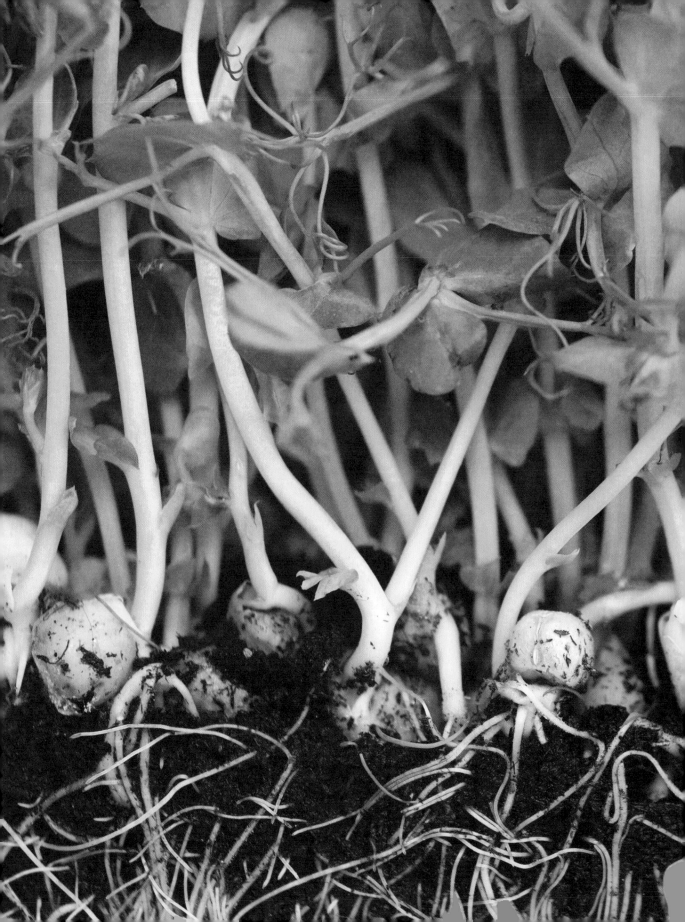

Vegetarian

141 recipes celebrating fresh, seasonal ingredients

Alice Hart

Photographs by Lisa Linder

MURDOCH BOOKS

Contents

This book is a celebration of the sublime ingredients that form the basis of a vegetarian diet.

Its purpose is to inspire even committed carnivores to eat without meat more often, and to demonstrate that meat-free cooking does not have to be worthy and dull. With a little coaxing and simple preparation, fresh and seasonal meat-free ingredients can result in dishes with deep and exciting flavours – with the added bonus that they are also nourishing.

You might not be a full-time vegetarian – you might just want to reduce the amount of meat you eat for nutritional or environmental reasons. Perhaps you feel that meat is not necessary or even practical to include in every meal. And that makes perfect sense. All too often, we view vegetables as an afterthought or a lame accompaniment to the main (meat) event. Reprising the days when vegetables, grains, legumes, herbs and fruit were central to meal times makes for a joyful way to cook.

And there has never been a better time to embrace meat-free cooking; our ancestors would be astonished at the variety of produce so readily available now. It's difficult not to be inspired by tomatoes all the colours of the sunset; sweet butternut squash with skins in palettes of purple through to slate-grey; and perfumeries of fragrant herbs. Meatless meals will also encourage you to explore new cuisines, new cooking methods and new ingredients. The recipes in this book draw inspiration from around the globe, from the fragrant, spice-laden dishes of North Africa to the clean, balanced flavours of Vietnam.

One of the intentions of this book is to demonstrate that vegetarian cooking need never be boring. If you find yourself trapped in a cooking rut, as most of us do occasionally, vegetarian cooking offers a means to haul yourself out – especially if you learn to eat with the seasons.

Chestnuts
(vacuum-packed or tins of purée)

Dried fruit

Rolled oats

Dried yeast

Dark chocolate

Vanilla pods and extract

Rosewater

Orange blossom water

Chutneys and preserves

Preserved lemons

Chilli sauce

Dried sea vegetables

Jars of antipasti vegetables

Mustards

Tahini paste

Nut butters

Sugars and honeys

Maple syrup

Vinegars and wine

Oils

Whole spices

Pomegranate molasses

Olives

Capers

Miso paste

Dried mushrooms

A variety of grains and rice

Flours

Coconut
(tins of milk, cream and flakes)

Soy sauce or tamari

Tinned tomatoes
(plus tomato purée and sugo or passata)

Pulses (dried and tinned)

Nuts and seeds

Dried pasta and noodles

Sea salt

Peppercorns
(black, white and Szechuan)

FOR THE FREEZER

Breadcrumbs

Kaffir lime leaves

Parmesan rinds

Wonton wrappers

Pastry

Peas

Edamame beans

Achieving balance

There is evidence that vegetarians suffer lower rates of coronary heart disease, obesity, hypertension and some other illnesses. This is because a non-meat diet tends to be rich in carbohydrates, omega-6 fatty acids, fibre, vitamins and minerals, and is low in saturated fat and cholesterol. It is also true that a vegetarian diet can sometimes lack protein, iron, zinc, Vitamin B12, calcium, omega-3 and some other minerals. But these requirements can be met if you eat a wide variety of food that includes fruit, vegetables, leafy greens, whole grains, nuts, seeds and legumes.

Obtaining protein

The average person should consume about 50g of protein per day and getting this in a vegetarian diet is easy. Pulses, nuts, seeds, soy, leafy green vegetables, eggs, cheese, milk, yoghurt, whole grains and cereals are all particularly high in protein. When you can, combine pulses with whole grains, nuts or seeds to form 'complete' protein, which contains all the amino acids your body needs.

THE FOLLOWING MENU
WOULD PROVIDE YOU
WITH YOUR DAILY PROTEIN
REQUIREMENT

start

GRANOLA WITH YOGHURT
(15G PROTEIN)

middle

HUMMUS WITH PITTA BREAD
AND SALAD
(15G PROTEIN)

between

BLACKBERRY MILKSHAKE
(10G PROTEIN)

end

RICOTTA GNOCCHI
WITH STIR-FRIED GREENS
(15G PROTEIN)

IDEALLY, AN AVERAGE
DAILY NON-MEAT
DIET SHOULD INCLUDE

three

SERVINGS OF STARCHY FOODS
LIKE GRAINS OR POTATOES

five

SERVINGS (AT LEAST) OF FRUIT
AND VEGETABLES

three

SERVINGS OF PROTEIN
LIKE PULSES, TOFU,
EGGS, NUTS OR SEEDS

two

SERVINGS OF DAIRY
LIKE MILK, CHEESE OR YOGHURT

three

SERVINGS (MAXIMUM)
OF OIL, FAT
OR SUGARY FOODS

Approximate protein equivalents in meat and vegetarian foods

2 large pork sausages = 240g red lentils = *20 grams protein*

 =  = *18 grams protein*

Half a can of tuna   3 large eggs

 = = *47 grams protein*

170g Steak   200g Peanuts

Conversion charts

LENGTH				WEIGHT				LIQUID	
cm	inches	cm	inches	g	oz	g	oz	ml	fl oz
2mm	1/16	13	5	5	1/8	150	5½	30	1
3mm	1/8	14	5½	10	¼	175	6	60	2
5mm	¼	15	6	15	½	200	7	80	2¾
8mm	3/8	16	6¼	20	¾	225	8	100	3½
1	½	17	6½	30	1	250	9	125	4
1.5	5/8	18	7	35	1¼	275	9¾	160	5½
2	¾	19	7½	40	1½	300	10½	185	6
2.5	1	20	8	50	1¾	350	12	200	7
3	1¼	21	8¼	55	2	375	13	250	9
4	1½	22	8½	60	2¼	400	14	300	10½
5	2	23	9	70	2½	450	1lb	350	12
6	2½	24	9½	80	2¾	500	1lb 2oz	375	13
7	2¾	25	10	85	3	550	1lb 4oz	400	14
7.5	3	30	12	90	3¼	600	1lb 5oz	500	17
8	3¼	35	14	100	3½	700	1lb 9oz	600	21
9	3½	40	16	115	4	800	1lb 12oz	650	22½
10	4	45	17¾	120	4¼	900	2lb	700	24
11	4¼	50	20	125	4½	1kg	2lb 3oz	750	26
12	4½			140	5			800	28
								1 litre	35
								1.25	44
								1.5	52

Seasonal eating

To get the maximum taste and nutritional benefit from vegetable
and freshly harvested. In other words, eat what the seasons delive

Spring

blood oranges, valencia oranges, peas, seville oranges, silverbeet
spinach, bananas, cherries, strawberries, beans, cumquats, leeks
honeydew melon, rockmelon, watermelon, lychees, grapefruit
lemons, mandarins, snow peas, sugar snap peas, broccoli, mangoes

Summer

aubergine, apricots, green beans, bananas, lychees, passionfruit
mangoes, melons, cucumber, leeks, squash, nectarine, pineapple
rambutan, tomatoes, valencia oranges, courgettes, white nectarines

Autumn

apples, bananas, potato, pumpkin, cumquat, custard apples, celery
tamarillos, figs, turnip, grapes, guava, papaya, rockmelon, lemons
limes, cauliflower, mandarins, mangosteen, nashi pears, brussels
sprouts, passionfruit, peaches, persimmons, capsicum, carrots, plums

Winter

apples, blood oranges, navel oranges, cumquat, nashi pears,
custard apples, Jerusalem artichoke, brussels sprouts, parsnip, peas
grapefruit, kale, okra, olives, kiwifruit, lemons, pears, beetroot, limes,
mandarins, cauliflower, persimmons, pineapple, quince, rhubarb.

and fruit, choose produce at optimum ripeness, which is locally grown
This table shows when produce is widely available and at its best.

angelos, tomatoes, artichokes, pineapple, asparagus, broad beans, cabbage, rhubarb, carrots, avocado, papaya, cucumber, lettuce, new potatoes, sweetcorn, cauliflower

asparagus, berries, cherries, currants, avocado, beans, borlotti beans, capsicum, celery, lettuce, peaches, radish, snow peas, sweetcorn, carrots, peas

pomegranate, squash, quinces, peas, cucumber, fennel, rambutan, rhubarb, valencia oranges, asian greens, aubergine, avocado, beans, beetroot, borlotti beans, cabbage, kiwifruit, leeks, lettuce, parsnip, mushrooms, onions, broccoli, silverbeet, spinach, sweet potato

angelos, asian greens, avocado, broccoli, carrot, celeriac, celery, fennel, horseradish, kohlrabi, leek, onion, potato, sweet potato, turnip, pumpkin, silverbeet, spinach, cabbage, swede

If you've chosen the meat-free path, you're in excellent company. The vegetarian Hall of Fame is filled with notable figures from across the centuries, including those from the arts, science, politics and religion.

DALAI LAMA

Drew Barrymore

CLINT EASTWOOD

BRAD PITT

TOLSTOY

Dizzy Gillespie

LEONARDO · DA · VINCI

Nathalie Baye

Stella McCartney

Paul Newman

TINA TURNER

VINCENT VAN GOGH

Essentials

Mushrooms and herbs

Use them because...

...if you're fond of meat but want to cut down, many mushrooms – notably gigantic field mushrooms – have a juicy, beefy quality that readily satisfies meat hankerings.

What to choose

Golden chanterelles, delicate enoki, shaggy chestnuts and tasty porcini are just a few examples, so celebrate the mushroom season and experiment. If culinary inspiration eludes you, just fry them in butter, garlic and herbs and enjoy them on toast. Heaven.

Don't forget

Herbs make cooking joyful, so treat them well. Robust rosemary, sage and bay *et al* need time to meld with companions in the pot, so add them early. The tender likes of basil, parsley and coriander go in at the end so their lovely oils don't dissipate away.

Vegetables and fruit

The golden rule
It's easy to take these vegetarian staples for granted, but try not to. Tricksy cooking and exotic varieties are not necessary – although I urge you to try the unfamiliar. Just buy seasonal, organic and ripe – and pause for thought if you're inclined to cooking autopilot. You don't have to steam them every time.

Have you tried…
…sprinkling simple veg with toasted seeds or topping with a knob of nut butter? It takes just moments to raise a dish from dull to delicious. And get to know your ingredients better. Salad leaves have wildly different personalities that you can't appreciate if you only know them as the contents of a plastic bag.

Kitchen essential
Soulful onion and her cousin, garlic, are kingpins of the vegetarian kitchen, and come into their own cooked gently in oil or butter, slow roasted or sweated in a pan. Pots of this sweet onion 'confit' will keep in the refrigerator ready for use in other dishes, or can be gobbled on bread with strong cheese.

And another thing
Your kitchen armoury is also lacking without lemon. A spritz here, a shower of zest there, can enliven, intensify or transform all manner of sweet and savoury dishes.

Culinary jewels

These delicious pods – including beans, lentils, peanuts, peas and soybeans – range from creamy white and dappled pink through to vivid red and smoky grey, like nature's own edible buttons and beads. Moreover, they're low in fat, high in protein and rich in nutrients, especially Vitamin Bs, iron and calcium. You can even enjoy the sensory pleasure of running them through your fingers. What's not to like?

Easy prepping

Cooking legumes isn't onerous. Really. Lentils and dried peas need no soaking. Pulses and beans do, for between 8–12 hours: just pour into a bowl of water before bed time and they'll be plump and ready to cook by morning. If you forget to soak them, cover with water and boil fiercely for a few minutes and set aside for 2 hours, then cook as normal. Don't bother salting the water – it toughens the skin.

Fabulous flavour

Robust herbs and aromatic vegetables added to the cooking water will enhance any type of legume: then mash, purée, mould into patties or add to salads and casseroles as you wish. Slippery with flavoursome oil or flecked with herbs and spices, legumes also hold their own in the flavour stakes.

Legumes

Nuts, seeds and oils

Did you know?

Nuts and seeds can be used in a range of culinary guises: toasted, ground, whole, sprouted, pressed into fragrant oil, whizzed into butter or transformed into milk. They can raise a dish from merely edible to one that sings with flavour, and add texture and depth of flavour to soups, casseroles and vegetables.

Noble feasting

They're tiny nutritional powerhouses: high in fibre, rich in nutrients and an excellent source of protein. The fat in nuts is now known to be largely mono or polyunsaturated – that's the good stuff – so they find favour with nutritionists. In any event, only modest amounts are needed to impart substance to cooking.

Why don't you try...

...using rich nut and seed oils in cold food, to annoint steamed veg, or added to hot dishes at the eleventh hour so the piquancy is not destroyed by cooking. (Do give special oils a place of honour in a dark cupboard to preserve freshness.) Or, whizz up cashews, almonds, macadamias, hazelnuts or pecans into creamy nut 'butters'. You can also blend various seeds to make mouth-tingling sprinkles.

Rice and grains

Cook because…

…they are comforting, economical, delicious and nutritious, and the starting point for countless dishes and products as varied as wine, milk, pasta and noodles.

Which rice?

Know the basics and you can choose the most appropriate type for your purpose. Thin and dainty long-grains, cooked *à point*, stay separated after cooking and make fluffy beds for curries and sauces. Short and medium-grains are plumper and starchier and stick together when cooked. Medium-grain is used in dishes like paella; short-grains makes creamy puddings and risottos.

Explore

Wholegrain rice and wild rice (a misnomer, as it's actually a grain) require more patience to cook than white rice, but the nutty, earthy flavours are worth the extra effort. Please forage in your health food shop and invite more of the unfamiliar grains into your kitchen: couscous, quinoa, amaranth, barley, bulgur…

Practical matters

Decanting rice and grain into airtight containers is not just for those who like their cupboards neat: it helps prevent them going rancid. Remember that cooked rice or grain left at room temperature can encourage bacteria to multiply, so serve when just cooked or refrigerate within 1 hour of cooking.

Dairy and eggs

Dairy treasures

Milk, butter, cream, cheese and yoghurt are the cornerstone ingredients of desserts and baking, but have a special place in vegetarian kitchens. A swirl of cream in soup, a gloss-inducing knob of butter in sauce, or parings of salty cheese on salad leaves: these add richness to food that might otherwise taste underwhelming. A globe of buratta or oven-baked ricotta will never leave a carnivore feeling deprived.

How about?

There are so many options. Some cheese is divine eaten raw, others are meltingly transformed by heat. Yoghurt can evolve into cheese such as labne: made in a muslin mould, it emerges striated with markings and is beautiful to behold as well as eat. Some ingredients in this book, such as Parmesan, are made from animal rennet, but alternatives suitable for vegetarians are readily available, so substitute if you wish.

Naturally convenient

Eggs add substance to a non-meat meal because they're packed with protein and are therefore filling. But they are senstive to heat and can be tricky to cook just so. The key is not to overcook: what point a luminous duck egg, served with celeriac soldiers for dunking, if the yolk is not gooey? For the best flavour, sunniest yolks and thickest whites, opt for free-range and organic eggs when possible.

Breakfast and Brunch

Chapter One

Almond milk has such a delicate, pure sweetness that it makes a beautiful porridge. I favour this raw, but on cold days hot porridge is really the only option, so heat it through gently. You can, of course, make porridge with other milks in place of the almond.

Almond milk and maple porridge

SERVES 4
PREPARATION TIME: 10 MINUTES
PLUS SOAKING TIME
COOKING TIME: 5 MINUTES

200g jumbo or rolled oats

½ a small cinnamon stick

500ml fresh, unsweetened almond milk

50g Medjool dates, stoned and chopped

50g flaked almonds, lightly toasted

a drizzle of maple syrup

If you can, soak the oats and cinnamon in half the almond milk the night before and keep in the refrigerator overnight. The oats will soften beautifully, enough in fact to be eaten just as they are with the dates, flaked almonds and a little maple syrup.

Assuming you are going to cook the porridge, place the soaked oats mixture in a saucepan with the remaining almond milk. Heat gently, stirring constantly for a few minutes until the porridge turns thick and creamy. Add a little more water if it looks too thick.

Remove the cinnamon stick and divide the oats between warmed bowls. Top with dates, almonds and a drizzle of amber maple syrup.

Versatile recipes such as this Antipodean favourite don't like to be pigeon-holed – herb and chilli-flecked baked ricotta can be breakfast, brunch, lunch or supper. The richly sweet and smoky compote is an excellent foil for the creamy cheese.

Baked ricotta with avocado

MAKES 4
PREPARATION TIME: 15 MINUTES
COOKING TIME: 20–25 MINUTES

500g ricotta, drained

2 tablespoons finely grated pecorino or Parmesan

1 red chilli, deseeded and finely chopped

2 tablespoons chopped basil

2 eggs, lightly beaten

extra virgin olive oil, to oil and drizzle

4 thick slices sourdough bread, toasted or griddled

2 ripe avocados, halved, stoned and sliced

1 bunch rocket

pepper compote (see page 242), to serve

Preheat the oven to 190°C (375°F/Gas 5). Beat the drained ricotta, pecorino or Parmesan, chilli, basil and eggs together and season with plenty of freshly ground black pepper and a little salt. Lightly oil 4 x 180ml pudding moulds or a small roasting dish and fill with the ricotta mixture. Bake for 20 minutes if using 4 moulds or about 25 minutes if using a single roasting dish. Leave to rest for a few minutes before running a knife around the edge and turning out.

Squish the baked ricotta onto the toasted sourdough, drizzle with olive oil and accompany with slices of avocado, rocket and smoky sweet pepper compote.

Breakfast and Brunch

Starting this recipe the night before will result in delicious plump oats that have soaked up all the milk. You could use walnut or soy milk here instead of cow's milk and mild honey instead of the agave nectar. Or just use diluted fruit juice instead.

Pear and walnut Bircher muesli

SERVES 2
PREPARATION TIME: 10 MINUTES
PLUS SOAKING TIME

2 firm pears, cored and coarsely grated

a squeeze of lemon

120g porridge oats

2 tablespoons mixed seeds

2 tablespoons chopped walnuts

1 tablespoon agave nectar

100ml fresh pear or apple juice

100ml milk or water

natural yoghurt, a few walnut halves and fresh pear slices, to serve

The night before, toss the grated pears with the lemon juice to stop them browning and combine with the oats, seeds and 1 tablespoon chopped walnuts in a large bowl. Add the agave nectar, pear or apple juice, and the milk or water. Stir well, cover and refrigerate.

The following morning, stir in a rounded spoonful of yoghurt and the remaining chopped walnuts. Divide between 2 bowls and top with extra yoghurt, walnut halves and fresh pear slices.

Breakfast and Brunch

Delicious nut milks, seed milks or nut-and-seed milks will last well for up to three days if kept chilled. Adding warm water and linseeds when blending the milk helps it to emulsify evenly, making it luxuriously creamy and smooth.

How to make nut milk

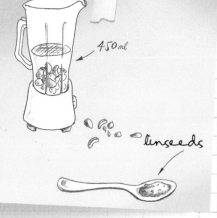

step 1.

Cover 100g of your choice of shelled nuts and/or seeds with plenty of cold water in a large bowl and leave to soak in a cool place overnight, or for at least 8 hours. The nuts and/or seeds will soften and plump up.

step 2.

If the milk is destined for a refined recipe, or if you want it to be particularly smooth, de-skin any nuts with skins remaining after their soaking time. Almonds are easy to skin by blanching – just nick with a knife and slip the white nuts out – but others such as walnuts and pecans will need to be rubbed vigorously with a clean tea towel to remove as much skin as possible.

step 3.

Place the soaked nuts in a blender with 450ml warm water. Add 1 tablespoon ground linseeds if you have them to help the milk emulsify, but this is not essential. Blend on a high speed for a couple of minutes until very smooth.

Brazil nuts, almonds, pumpkins seeds, sesame seeds, peanuts, walnuts, cashews, sunflower seeds, macadamias, hazelnuts and pistachios are all good choices on their own or in combination, but do make sure your nuts and seeds are unroasted and buy organic if possible.

twist   squeeze

2 layers   nut milk

step 5.

Finish by gathering the muslin up and squeezing over the bowl to extract the liquid from the solids.

dates

sugar

honey

step 6.

You can sweeten the creamy nut milk with 1–2 tablespoons (or more to taste) of maple syrup, mild honey, unrefined sugar or a few stoned dates. To do this, return the milk to the rinsed blender, add the sweetener and blend again. Add nothing more if the milk is to be used in savoury recipes, or in smoothies or shakes, as they will be sweetened as you make them. You could also add flavourings like vanilla seeds, ground cinnamon, ground nutmeg or cocoa powder at this stage. Dilute the milk to taste with extra water if you wish. Chill the milk or use when warm.

step 4.

Line a sieve with 2 layers of muslin cloth and set over a bowl. Pour the nut milk through slowly to filter out the remaining nut pieces.

If you can spare 15 minutes, delicious melty panini can be yours for breakfast instead of a sad bowl of bran flakes. Wrap them in paper to keep warm for 10 minutes – this will give you just enough time to run for the bus before you tuck in.

Toasted goat's curd and charred tomato panini

MAKES 2 PANINI
READY IN 15 MINUTES

2 small ciabatta rolls

1 large, ripe tomato, sliced 5mm thick

75g soft, mild goat's curd

3 tarragon sprigs, leaves only

olive oil, for drizzling

Split each ciabatta in half horizontally. If the rolls are very thick, slice into 3 and save the middle section for breadcrumbs, leaving you with thin top and bottom pieces.

Place a non-stick frying pan over a high heat until smoking hot. Add the tomato to the pan – making sure the end pieces are cut side down. Leave undisturbed for a minute before reducing the heat to medium and leaving to char for a further minute or so. Remove from the pan with a spatula and set aside.

Beat the goat's curd and tarragon together and spread over the bottom ciabatta halves. Put the charred tomatoes onto the curd mixture, and place the remaining ciabatta halves on top, pressing them down firmly. Drizzle the tops and bottoms of the panini with a little olive oil.

Switch on an electric sandwich press if you have one, or place a sturdy griddle pan on the stove to heat. If using a sandwich press, place the panini on the ridged hotplate and press down the cover to flatten the panini as they cook. They will need at least 2 minutes, or according to your machine's instructions. If using a griddle, place the panini in the hot pan and rest a heavy frying pan on top to weigh them down. Cook over a medium-high heat for a minute or 2 then remove the frying pan, turn the panini over and replace the pan to weigh them down for a further minute. Whichever way you cook them, eat while they're still warm.

Breakfast and Brunch

The blackberry milkshake is arguably the less virtuous recipe here, but is so delicious. Use frozen yoghurt – plain, vanilla or berry – or if your milkshake is more of a treat, replace the yoghurt with a scoop of vanilla ice cream and a couple of teaspoons of sugar instead of honey. Linseeds will help the mango and cashew smoothie emulsify.

Blackberry milkshake, mango and cashew smoothie

MAKES 2 OF EACH
PREPARATION TIME: 10 MINUTES FOR EACH
PLUS SOAKING TIME FOR THE SMOOTHIE

FOR THE BLACKBERRY
MILKSHAKE:

1 vanilla pod

300g blackberries, fresh or frozen

a generous drizzle of mild runny honey

2 large scoops frozen yoghurt

400ml milk, chilled

FOR THE MANGO AND
CASHEW SMOOTHIE:

100g unsalted cashews

300ml water, chilled

1 ripe mango, stoned and flesh chopped

1 small banana

3 ice cubes, crushed

1 tablespoon golden linseeds

1 tablespoon porridge oats

Blackberry milkshake

Split the vanilla pod along its length and scrape the seeds into a blender with the tip of the knife. (You can use the empty pod to flavour a bag of sugar in your store cupboard.) Add the rest of the ingredients to the blender and simply blitz together. Immediately divide between 2 tall glasses. That's it.

Mango and cashew smoothie

Start the evening before: soak the cashews in plenty of cold water and leave overnight to soften. The following morning, drain the cashews and place in a blender with 100ml chilled water. Blitz until a paste forms, then pour in a further 200ml chilled water while the motor is running to form rich, smooth milk. This will take a couple of minutes. Throw in the remaining ingredients and blitz for at least another minute until smooth. Pour into 2 tall or 4 small glasses and drink straight away.

Make a batch of granola and you'll be set for breakfast for a couple of weeks – or you can simply snack on it from the jar. Any seasonal fruit compote will be a lovely accompaniment, but Barbie-pink rhubarb, roasted with vanilla sugar and a splash of water until tender, is perfect.

Toasted honey and pumpkin seed granola with yoghurt

MAKES 12 BOWLFULS
PREPARATION TIME: 10 MINUTES
COOKING TIME: 30 MINUTES

500g jumbo or rolled oats

2 tablespoons wheat germ (optional)

100g pumpkin seeds

50g sunflower seeds

50g sesame seeds

50g desiccated coconut (unsweetened)

100ml pumpkin seed oil or sunflower oil

120g mild, runny honey

natural yoghurt, to serve

Preheat the oven to 150°C (300°F/Gas 2). Line 2 baking trays with non-stick baking paper and combine all ingredients (except yoghurt) in a large bowl, tossing together until evenly coated with oil and honey. Spread over the lined trays and bake for about 30 minutes, stirring the mixture at least 3 times to ensure everything browns evenly. The granola should be golden and smell toasted. Cool, then transfer to airtight jars. Serve in bowls with yoghurt and/or milk and perhaps some fruit compote or a little fresh fruit. Or eat dry as a snack.

VARIATIONS

Apricot and almond
Use maple syrup and almond oil in place of the honey and pumpkin seed oil, and chopped almonds instead of pumpkin seeds. Replace the coconut with 100g chopped dried apricots, adding them for the last 10 minutes of cooking.

Cherry and coconut
Increase the coconut to 75g and use sunflower oil not pumpkin seed oil. Add 100g chopped pistachio nuts and omit the pumpkin and sunflower seeds. Add 100g dried cherries for the last 10 minutes of cooking and serve with cherries.

Chocolate and fig
Replace the honey with light agave nectar and the seeds with 100g flaked almonds. Add 100g dried figs to the granola for the last 10 minutes of cooking. When cooled completely stir in 100g dark chocolate, chopped small. Eat with cold milk or as it is.

Of course you can buy yoghurt from the supermarket or health food shop, but there is something special about the yoghurt you make yourself. Make sure you keep all your utensils scrupulously clean during this process so you don't encourage bad bacteria.

How to make yoghurt

step 1.

Bring 500ml milk to the boil in a saucepan. Use whole, semi or skimmed milk, depending on how rich you would like the finished yoghurt to be.

step 2.

Immediately set aside to cool until the temperature falls to 45°C (115°F). If you don't have a thermometer, test the temperature with a clean finger – if you can keep your finger in the milk for 10 seconds the temperature will be about right.

step 3.

Discard any skin from the milk's surface and add 2 tablespoons of the milk to a small bowl containing a heaped tablespoon of live (cultured) yoghurt that you have bought or made earlier.

fresh milk

Skimmed milk can be used as effectively as full fat milk but full fat milk will produce thicker yoghurt. Whatever kind of milk you choose to use, yoghurt is a healthy source of protein, calcium, magnesium and other essential vitamins, whose active bacterial cultures aid in digestion.

warm milk mix

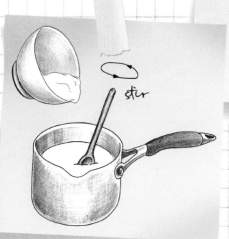

stir

8 hours

step 5.

Pour the warm milk mix into a lidded container – a Tupperware or clean ice cream tub is ideal.

step 6.

Place the lid on, wrap the container in a towel or blanket and leave in a warm place such as an airing cupboard for about 8 hours. You should now have a tub of yoghurt! Keep chilled from this point to prevent the milk souring any further and use within a week or so. You can use this live yoghurt to make your next batch.

step 4.

Scrape the milk and yoghurt mixture back into the saucepan and stir well.

Small Bites

Chapter Two

These are delicate little bites but the cheese does lend them substance. Chard is related to beetroot and has an earthier taste than spinach. But if you want to, you could just use spinach leaves instead of chard here, in which case use 150g spinach, wilt as per the instructions for the chard, and continue with the recipe.

Chard and Brie mini muffins

MAKES 12–24
PREPARATION TIME: 20 MINUTES
COOKING TIME: 15 MINUTES

25g butter, melted, plus extra for greasing

150g rainbow or Swiss chard, leaves washed and shredded, stalks reserved

190g self-raising flour

2 tablespoons finely grated Parmesan

a good grating of nutmeg

175ml milk

1 small egg, beaten

75g Brie or Camembert, cubed

Preheat the oven to 190°C (375°F/Gas 5). Grease a 12-hole standard muffin tin or a 24-hole mini-muffin tin with a little butter or line with paper cases if you prefer.

Chop the chard stalks and steam for 4 minutes, add the chard leaves and steam for a further minute or so. Turn into a clean tea towel and squeeze out any excess water.

Mix the flour, 1 tablespoon Parmesan, a pinch of salt and the nutmeg in a bowl. In a separate bowl, beat the milk, melted butter and egg together. Tip the milk mixture into the flour bowl and mix a couple of times. Now add the cooked chard stalks, chard leaves and the Brie or Camembert. Don't over-mix or the muffins will be tough – a few lumps are just fine.

Spoon the mixture into the holes of the muffin tin, sprinkle with the remaining Parmesan and bake for about 15 minutes until risen and golden. Cool on wire racks or eat warm.

Small Bites

Even at their best, falafel can be on the heavy side of vegetarian fare, and deep-frying them can be a faff. Not so here. Sweet roast squash combines beautifully with the spices and nutty chickpeas to make falafel with a lighter texture and a more rounded flavour.

Butternut squash and coriander falafel with cucumber yoghurt

MAKES ABOUT 16
REPARATION TIME: 20 MINUTES
PLUS CHILLING AND STANDING TIME
COOKING TIME: 50 MINUTES

FOR THE FALAFEL:

500g butternut squash, deseeded and cubed

2 tablespoons olive oil

300g cooked chickpeas, or 1 x 400g tin, drained

2 garlic cloves, roughly chopped

½ teaspoon bicarbonate of soda

1 small bunch parsley, leaves only, chopped

1 small bunch coriander, leaves only, chopped

1 teaspoon ground coriander

1 teaspoon ground cumin

FOR THE YOGHURT:

½ cucumber, peeled, deseeded and coarsely grated

300g thick natural yoghurt

1 tablespoon lemon juice

Preheat the oven to 200°C (400°F/Gas 6). Toss the butternut squash with 1 tablespoon olive oil and season well. Spread out on a baking tray and roast for about 35 minutes until soft and caramelised. Set aside to cool.

Place the well-drained chickpeas in a food processor with the garlic, bicarbonate of soda, parsley, fresh and ground coriander and cumin. Pulse the machine, stopping every now and then to scrape down the sides with a spatula, until the mixture forms a rough paste. Tip into a large bowl and season well with salt and pepper.

Crush the roast squash with a fork until very roughly mashed and add to the chickpeas. Fold everything together. Chill for 30 minutes if you have time.

Scoop dessertspoonfuls onto a baking tray lined with non-stick baking paper and space out well. Drizzle with the remaining olive oil and bake at 200°C (400°F/Gas 6) for 15–20 minutes until golden underneath.

To make the cucumber yoghurt, scoop the grated cucumber into a colander or sieve, sprinkle with salt and set aside for 20 minutes. Rinse and squeeze dry with a clean tea towel. Stir into the yoghurt with the lemon juice and some salt and pepper to taste. Serve with the falafel, adding flatbread and salad if this is more of a sit-down affair.

Black vinegar should be easy to source at Chinese food shops, but if you don't have the means or inclination, try two tablespoons of rice vinegar instead. The wonton wrappers can be a little fiddly, but it gets easier as you go along, and the results are well worth it.

Potsticker dumplings with black vinegar dipping sauce

MAKES ABOUT 36
PREPARATION TIME: 20 MINUTES
COOKING TIME: 25 MINUTES

FOR THE DIPPING SAUCE:

4 tablespoons light soy sauce

3 tablespoons black vinegar

1 teaspoon caster sugar

2 tablespoons chilli oil

FOR THE POTSTICKERS:

100g Savoy cabbage, sliced wafer thin

3 tablespoons vegetable oil

2 garlic cloves, crushed

4cm piece ginger, finely chopped

150g shiitake mushrooms, finely chopped

3 spring onions, finely sliced

3 carrots, grated

1 large bunch coriander, finely chopped

1 teaspoon white pepper

1 tablespoon light soy sauce

1 teaspoon sesame oil

36 round wonton wrappers

Start with the dipping sauce: combine all the ingredients and set aside.

Finely chop the cabbage slices. Place 1 tablespoon vegetable oil, garlic and ginger in a large wok and set over a medium heat. Cook, stirring, for a minute until the mixture sizzles, then add the chopped cabbage, mushrooms, spring onions and carrots. Stir-fry for 5 minutes or so until the mixture softens and any liquid in the pan evaporates.

Remove from the heat and stir in the coriander followed by the white pepper, soy sauce, sesame oil and a generous pinch of salt. Allow to cool a little.

Place 2 teaspoons of this filling in the middle of a wonton wrapper and brush the border with water. Fold over to form a half-moon shape, pleating the edges together about 5 times as you go. Press the edges firmly to seal completely. Sit the dumplings so the seam is vertical and the base is flat, on a baking tray lined with non-stick baking paper. Cover with a damp tea towel as you make them.

Now, pour 1 tablespoon of the remaining oil into a large non-stick frying pan and set over a medium heat. Add half the dumplings to the pan, flat base down. Fry them undisturbed for about 2 minutes until golden underneath. Pour 200ml water into the pan, bring to the boil then reduce the heat slightly. Cover with a lid or a large baking tray and simmer for about 8 minutes, or until no liquid remains in the pan. Serve straight away with half the dipping sauce and repeat the cooking process with the remaining dumplings.

Small Bites

Panelle are traditional Italian chickpea pancakes that are made in a very similar way to firm polenta – season the batter well and get the panelle good and golden in the pan. There might be extra caponata left over, but it keeps beautifully, chilled, for up to two weeks.

Robust caponata spooned onto panelle

MAKES ABOUT 25
PREPARATION TIME: 25 MINUTES
PLUS COOLING TIME
COOKING TIME: 50 MINUTES

FOR THE CAPONATA:

2 medium vine tomatoes

2 aubergines, cubed

100ml olive oil

1 red onion, finely sliced

2 celery sticks, sliced

50g green olives, stoned and halved

2 tablespoons white wine vinegar

2 tablespoons caster sugar

2 tablespoons pine nuts, lightly toasted

FOR THE PANELLE:

4 tablespoons extra virgin olive oil

150g chickpea flour

parsley sprigs, to serve

Nick the bases of the tomatoes and cover with boiling water. Leave for a minute then drain and peel the skin away. Chop the tomato flesh.

In a large frying pan, fry the aubergines in 75ml of the olive oil, stirring until golden all over. Scoop out and set aside on a plate. Turn down the heat, add the onion and remaining olive oil to the pan and sauté until golden. Add the celery and continue to cook for a minute, followed by the tomatoes, olives, vinegar, sugar and pine nuts. Simmer gently for 15 minutes. Cool to room temperature and season to taste.

For the panelle, pour 390ml water into a saucepan with 1 tablespoon of the olive oil and add the chickpea flour in a steady stream, whisking as you go. Cook over a medium heat, stirring constantly with a wooden spoon, until the mixture thickens – this will take longer than you think, so allow 20 minutes. Lay a piece of baking paper on a chopping board, and spread the thickened mixture onto it; it should be just over 1cm thick.

Leave until cool and firm, then cut into small squares or diamond shapes and fry in the remaining olive oil until golden and crisp on both sides. Spoon a little caponata onto each panelle, add a parsley sprig, and serve.

If the idea of perfect little spheres offends you, try crushing the coated cheese slightly with the back of a fork. Drizzle the bites with olive oil and offer toasted flatbreads to scoop them up.

Roasted red pepper and goat's cheese bites

MAKES ABOUT 30
PREPARATION TIME: 15 MINUTES

2 roasted red peppers in olive oil, drained and chopped

250g soft goat's cheese, curd cheese or labne (see page 50)

2 tablespoons coriander seeds, toasted and crushed

1 teaspoon black pepper, crushed

4 tablespoons finely chopped coriander

extra virgin olive oil, to cover (optional)

Stir the chopped peppers into the cheese and roll into heaped teaspoon-sized balls.

Combine the coriander seeds, black pepper and chopped coriander with a pinch of salt and spread out on a large plate. Roll the cheese rounds in this mixture to coat.

Serve as they are with crisp flatbread or if you'd rather save them for another time, place in a bowl or jar and cover with extra virgin olive oil. Chill and eat within a couple of weeks.

This cheese looks beautiful and tastes even better. Leave to marinate for at least a day before eating in salads or on fresh bread. It will last in its oil for up to two weeks if you keep it chilled.

How to make labne

plain yoghurt

500g

muslin

step 1.

Rinse and wring out a sheet of muslin and use it to line a colander or sieve, ensuring excess cloth overhangs the edges. Set the colander or sieve in or over a mixing bowl.

step 2.

Stir ½ teaspoon salt into 500g plain yoghurt (or 3 tablespoons caster sugar if you would prefer a sweet cheese). You can also add flavourings and spices at this stage: citrus zest, a teaspoon of crushed coriander or cumin seeds, a pinch of dried chilli, chopped herbs or vanilla seeds scraped from a pod.

yoghurt

cloth

step 3.

Spoon the yoghurt into the cloth and fold the overhanging edges over.

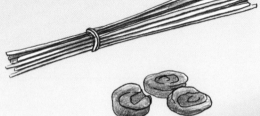

Ingredients for your labne include: natural yoghurt, salt, caster sugar, lemon, dried apricots, coriander seeds, cumin seeds, dried chilli, thyme and other fresh herbs, olive oil.

caster sugar

unwrap

15½ hours

plate

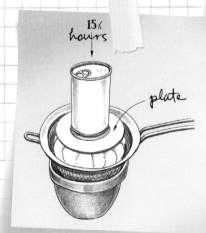

step 4.

Set a small plate on top and weigh down with an unopened tin or bottle. You will not need much weight to press the yoghurt. Leave in a cool place for up to 15 hours.

step 5.

The longer you leave the cheese, the firmer it will be. To speed up the process, gently squeeze the muslin to force extra water out of the cheese. Carefully unwrap the cheese and turn onto a plate. It will have a domed shape with beautiful markings from the cloth.

add olive oil, herbs and seeds

step 6.

Use as it is or beat in extra herbs for a savoury version, or chopped dried fruit for a sweet cheese. The drained whey can be used to make bread, or discarded. The cheese will keep, chilled and covered, for up to 4 days but you can also form it into walnut-sized balls and place in a sterilised jar. Pour over enough extra virgin olive oil to cover and add a few robust herb stalks such as rosemary or thyme, and perhaps a few coriander seeds. Leave the cheese to marinate for at least a day before eating in salads or on fresh bread.

Any edible squash blossoms would be perfect here, but if none are available, a delicate seasonal vegetable would be lovely, such as young, fresh asparagus. Enjoy these warm or cold.

Courgette blossom and tomato frittatas

MAKES 12
PREPARATION TIME: 10 MINUTES
COOKING TIME: 15–20 MINUTES

2 tablespoons olive oil, plus extra for oiling

1 fat garlic clove, crushed

15g butter

150g cherry tomatoes

12 courgette flowers

6 large eggs

100ml single cream

a small handful of basil leaves

Preheat the oven to 200°C (400°F/Gas 6). Oil a 12-hole non-stick muffin tin with olive oil.

Pour the 2 tablespoons olive oil into a frying pan and add the garlic. Place over a low heat and cook gently, stirring, for a couple of minutes. Turn the heat up and add the butter and tomatoes. Cook for a couple of minutes then add the courgette flowers. Cook for a brief minute to wilt them then remove the pan from the heat.

Beat the eggs, cream and basil together and season well. Spoon this mixture into the holes of the muffin tin, top with some of the garlicky tomato and a wilted courgette flower.

Bake for 15–20 minutes until puffed up and golden. Leave to stand for a few minutes before turning out.

This full-flavour trio is dedicated to all things mellow and earthy: roast garlic is subtle, carrots are sweet, tahini and lentils are nutty. I serve this in bowls, with a pile of crisp toasts sitting alongside.

Puy lentil hummus, carrot and cumin hummus, garlic toasts

SERVES 4
PREPARATION TIME: 20 MINUTES
COOKING TIME: 1 HOUR 15 MINUTES

FOR THE ROAST GARLIC TOASTS:

1 bulb garlic, unpeeled

olive oil, for drizzling

2 seeded bread rolls

FOR THE LENTIL HUMMUS:

175g Puy lentils, rinsed and drained

4 sun-dried tomatoes in oil

2 tablespoons chopped parsley

1 tablespoon lemon juice

FOR THE CARROT HUMMUS:

2 large carrots, sliced

2 tablespoons olive oil

300g cooked chickpeas or 1 x 400g tin, well drained

1 tablespoon light tahini paste

a pinch of ground cardamom

1 tablespoon lemon juice

Preheat the oven to 200°C (400°F/Gas 6). Slice the top off the garlic bulb to just expose the cloves. Drizzle with olive oil and wrap loosely in foil, sealing securely. Bake for 30 minutes or so until soft.

When cooked, squeeze the garlic cloves from the bulb into a bowl, mash with a fork and add a good drizzle of olive oil and a pinch of salt Cut the bread rolls into slices 5mm thick at most, and brush both sides with the roast garlic mixture. Space out on a baking sheet and place in the oven for a few minutes until just turning golden at the edges.

Cover the lentils with 500ml cold water in a saucepan and bring to the boil. Simmer gently for about 30 minutes, stirring occasionally until the liquid has been absorbed. Transfer to a blender and add a teaspoon of the roast garlic mixture, the sun-dried tomatoes and a drizzle of their oil, parsley and lemon juice. Blend to a rough purée, adding a little water if necessary, and season to taste with salt and pepper.

Place the carrots in a separate saucepan and enough water to cover them. Add the 2 tablespoons olive oil and a pinch of salt and bring to the boil. Simmer for about 8 minutes until the carrots are tender. Pour the whole lot into a blender with the chickpeas, tahini, cardamom, lemon juice and a teaspoon of the roast garlic mixture. Whizz until puréed. Serve with the toasts and lentil hummus.

Serrano chillies are the longish, pointed variety commonly available in supermarkets: use red or green in the guacamole as you wish, but go easy if they are extra fiery. This dish also works well with large potatoes, and their cooking times have also been included in this recipe.

Cumin potato skins and guacamole salsa

SERVES 4
PREPARATION TIME: 20 MINUTES
COOKING TIME: 50–60 MINUTES

FOR THE POTATO SKINS:

15 new potatoes or small waxy potatoes

3 tablespoons olive oil

2 teaspoons cumin seeds

FOR THE SALSA:

½ teaspoon cumin seeds

4 large, ripe avocados, halved and stoned

2 ripe tomatoes, deseeded and diced

½ red onion, finely chopped

2 serrano chillies, deseeded and finely chopped

juice of 1 large or 2 small limes

2 tablespoons chopped coriander

Preheat the oven to 180°C (350°F/Gas 4). Scrub the potatoes lightly if they look muddy, sprinkle with a little salt and bake for 50–60 minutes until tender. Set aside to cool a little. Cut each potato in half and scoop out the flesh. This is perfect for turning into mash (just beat in butter, salt and milk to taste), for making vegetable patties or even adding to bread dough before baking. Drizzle the potato skins with the olive oil and rub in the cumin seeds and a generous sprinkle of salt. Space out on a baking tray and bake for 15 minutes or so until crisp and golden.

Meanwhile, to make the salsa, toast the cumin seeds in a dry frying pan until fragrant. Crush roughly. Mash the avocados with a fork, but you don't want them smooth; the aim is to leave a lot of texture. Stir in the remaining ingredients including the toasted cumin seeds and season to taste.

Serve the crisp potato skins alongside the salsa, with a spoon for scooping, or spoon the salsa into each potato half and eat before they soften.

This recipe can be adapted for large potatoes: just bake 4 potatoes for 1 hour 20 minutes then halve, scoop out the flesh and cut the skin into strips before serving with the salsa.

Small Bites

These dear little sizzling pancakes are close cousins of the much larger banh xeo of southern Vietnam. They originate from Hue in central Vietnam and would ordinarily contain some meat or seafood, but mushrooms make a fine substitute. It's great finger food.

Mushroom banh khoai

MAKES ABOUT 18
PREPARATION TIME: 20 MINUTES
COOKING TIME: 25 MINUTES
PLUS 3–4 MINUTES PER PANCAKE

60g dried mung beans

230g rice flour

½ teaspoon ground turmeric

2 eggs, beaten

1 tablespoon caster sugar

150g mixed exotic mushrooms (such as oyster, enoki and shiitake), torn if large

1 fat garlic clove, finely chopped

vegetable oil, for frying

150g bean sprouts

2 spring onions, sliced

TO SERVE:

soft lettuce leaves and/or rice paper rounds

soft herbs

sliced cucumber

ginger and lime dipping sauce (see page 244)

Soak the mung beans in plenty of cold water for at least 30 minutes or overnight if that's easier. Drain, then steam the beans over simmering water for 15–20 minutes until tender.

Meanwhile, mix the flour and turmeric in a bowl and gradually whisk in 320ml cold water, then the beaten eggs, sugar and a large pinch of salt. Set aside for 10 minutes so the flour can expand and thicken the batter slightly.

Stir-fry the mushrooms and garlic in a little oil over a very high heat for a couple of minutes. Season with salt and pepper and set aside.

For each pancake, place a 12cm blini pan or mini frying pan over a medium-high heat and add a tablespoon of vegetable oil. The pan should be hot before you add just enough batter to coat the base – it should sizzle. Scatter with a few steamed mung beans, a spoonful of the cooked mushrooms, a few bean sprouts and a few spring onion slices. Fry for a couple of minutes until the edges and base are crisp. Fold the pancake in half with a spatula and slide out of the pan. Wrap the cooked banh khoai in lettuce leaves or rice paper and dunk in the dipping sauce between bites. Serve hot with the herb leaves and cucumber.

Small Bites

Don't be scared off by the prospect of sprouting the chickpeas yourself before making this lovely dish. The process is really very easy and the sprouts will be ready to use within a few days. The added bonus is that they're nutritious as well as tasty.

Sprouted chickpea and avocado hummus

SERVES 4
PREPARATION TIME: 10 MINUTES
PLUS SOAKING AND SPROUTING TIME

300g dried chickpeas

2 tablespoons light tahini paste

1 garlic clove, crushed

1 teaspoon sea salt

juice of 1 lime

1 ripe avocado, halved, stoned and chopped

a little paprika and avocado oil, to finish (optional)

vegetable crudités and warm flatbread, to serve

Soak the chickpeas in plenty of cold water for 12–48 hours. Leave them out of direct sunlight in a cool place. Drain the chickpeas and rinse well. Spread out on a tray or large plate and stand in a cool place (again out of direct sunlight) for 2 or 3 days while they sprout. Rinse them with cold water and drain well at least twice a day to stop them going mouldy.

Bring a large saucepan of water to the boil and plunge the sprouted chickpeas into the pan. Remove from the heat, leave for a minute then drain in a colander and refresh the sprouts under cold running water to take away any bitterness.

Place the drained sprouts in a food processor or blender with the remaining ingredients and 100–200ml water, as needed, to make a smooth paste. You will need to blend the hummus for 3–4 minutes, scraping down the sides with a spatula every now and then, until it is velvety smooth.

Serve with crisp vegetable crudités and plenty of warm flatbread for scooping.

This is a truly beautiful starter or picnic recipe – it's light and incredibly pretty. If you can make it a couple of days ahead and leave the terrine mould weighed down with unopened tins, the flavours will mellow and it will slice like a dream. Serve with toasted flatbread.

Sunblush terrine

SERVES 4
PREPARATION TIME: 25 MINUTES
PLUS PRESSING AND CHILLING TIME
COOKING TIME: 25 MINUTES

4 red peppers, halved and deseeded

2 yellow peppers, halved and deseeded

2 orange peppers, halved and deseeded

olive oil, for roasting

2 courgettes, very finely sliced lengthways

1 teaspoon fennel seeds, lightly crushed

a bunch of spring onions

50g sunblush or sun-dried tomatoes, drained and roughly chopped

500g ricotta

2 tablespoons shredded fennel herb or dill

½ garlic clove, crushed

wild rocket (optional), to serve

Preheat the oven to 220°C (425°F/Gas 7). Cut the peppers into quarters and toss with a little olive oil. Spread out on a large oiled baking tray, skin sides up. Roast for 20 minutes or so until the peppers are soft and blackened. Tip into a bowl, cover with a plate and set aside while the steam loosens the skins.

Meanwhile, heat a griddle pan until smoking. Toss the courgettes in a bowl with a little olive oil and the fennel seeds, and season with salt and pepper. Griddle the slices in batches – they should be spread out in a single layer – for a minute or less on each side, until marked and just soft. Remove to a plate.

Now toss the spring onions in a little olive oil, season and griddle for a couple of minutes, turning with tongs, until soft and a little blackened on all sides.

Once the peppers have cooled, slip their skins off. Combine the sunblush tomatoes with the ricotta, shredded fennel or dill, and garlic. Season well with salt and pepper.

Line an 11 x 24cm terrine mould with clingfilm, and line this with the courgette strips, overlapping them so they completely cover the sides and base. Leave any extra overhanging the edges. Put one-third of the peppers in the base of the terrine mould and cover these with half the ricotta mixture. Pack the spring onions lengthways on top and add half the remaining peppers, then the rest of the ricotta. Finish with the last of the peppers. Fold over any overhanging courgettes, cover with the clingfilm and weigh down with a couple of unopened tins. Chill for at least 5 hours or leave overnight if you can. Turn out, unwrap and slice. Serve with wild rocket (if using).

The dense and salty feta is tempered with creamy fromage frais and balanced by the honey-sweet pumpkin. The spicy harissa paste – a hot North African chilli sauce – adds a touch of fire to these crisp tarts.

Spiced pumpkin and feta puff pastry tarts

SERVES 4
PREPARATION TIME: 20 MINUTES
COOKING TIME: 35–40 MINUTES

400g pumpkin, deseeded and sliced

1 tablespoon olive oil

100g feta

1 tablespoon harissa

1 egg, beaten

2 tablespoons fromage frais

a little flour, for dusting

375g all-butter puff pastry

4 thyme sprigs, leaves stripped

Preheat the oven to 200°C (400°F/Gas 6). Toss the pumpkin with the olive oil, season with salt and pepper and spread out on a roasting tray. Cook for about 25 minutes until tender. Set aside to cool a little. Reduce the oven temperature to 190°C (375°F/Gas 5).

Cut half the feta into small cubes and crumble the rest. Beat the harissa, egg, fromage frais and crumbled feta together in a bowl and season with pepper and just a little salt (the cheese is already salty).

Lightly flour a work surface and roll out the pastry until it's about 20 x 30cm. Trim with a sharp knife so the sides are straight, and cut into 12 equal-sized rectangles. Space out on a baking tray. Spoon a little of the harissa mixture on the centre of each piece of pastry and top with pumpkin and feta cubes. Sprinkle with the thyme and bake for 15–20 minutes until puffed and golden. Serve warm, or cool the tarts on a wire rack.

To make a fresh chutney to go with the pakora, blend a large handful of chopped mint with a small handful of chopped coriander. Chop a small red onion and a couple of green chillies and add to the herbs with a squeeze of lime, a generous splash of water and a pinch of salt.

Spring vegetable pakoras

MAKES ABOUT 20
PREPARATION TIME: 20 MINUTES
COOKING TIME: 2–3 MINUTES

½ teaspoon cumin seeds, crushed

½ teaspoon coriander seeds, crushed

½ teaspoon ground turmeric

½ teaspoon chilli powder

½ teaspoon salt

¼ teaspoon baking powder

200g gram or chickpea flour

1 litre vegetable oil, for deep-frying

200g purple sprouting or tenderstem broccoli, roughly chopped

100g shelled peas

5 spring onions, roughly chopped

Mix the cumin, coriander, turmeric, chilli powder, salt, baking powder and gram flour together in a large bowl and gradually whisk in 200ml cold water to form a batter.

Heat the oil in a deep saucepan or wok until it reaches 180°C (350°F/Gas 4). If you don't have a thermometer drop a little batter into the pan – it should sizzle and dance immediately if hot enough.

Add the broccoli, peas and spring onions to the batter and stir to coat. Drop tablespoons of this mixture into the hot oil, being careful not to overcrowd the pan. Deep-fry for 2–3 minutes until golden brown. Lift out with a slotted spoon and drain on absorbent kitchen paper. Serve immediately, perhaps with the fresh chutney described above.

Preparing this dish is just so simple and the real boon is that only three ingredients are needed for the terrine. It's sublime served with mayonnaise, but the terrine also works well with a basic vinaigrette.

Pressed leek terrine and Dijon mayonnaise

SERVES 8
PREPARATION TIME: 20 MINUTES
PLUS PRESSING AND CHILLING TIME
COOKING TIME: 10–12 MINUTES

1.2kg young, slender leeks

½ small bunch chives, finely chopped

100g fromage blanc or curd cheese

FOR THE DIJON MAYONNAISE:

4 tablespoons mayonnaise (see page 236) or quality bought mayonnaise

1 teaspoon Dijon mustard

Line a standard terrine mould or 500g loaf tin with clingfilm. Trim the leeks to roughly the same length as the terrine mould, leaving a little green at the ends. Rinse them well under cold running water to wash away any grit. Drop into a large pan of salted, boiling water and simmer for 10–12 minutes until completely tender to the point of a knife. Drain and leave to cool slightly.

Sprinkle the base of the terrine mould with a teaspoon of chopped chives then cover with leeks, laying them lengthways and alternating white and green ends. Cover with a few evenly spaced teaspoonfuls of cheese. Season well with pepper, a little salt, and more chopped chives. Keep layering until all the ingredients have been used, finishing with a snug layer of leeks. Cover with clingfilm and weigh down with a couple of unopened tins. Chill for at least 4 hours or preferably overnight. Combine the mayonnaise and mustard.

Using a sharp, serrated knife slice the terrine very carefully and transfer to serving plates. You should get at least 8 slices from 1 terrine. Serve with the Dijon mayonnaise.

Do make sure the oil is hot enough before you start frying these tasty vegetable morsels. The tempura should be crisp and light, never greasy, so tepid oil just won't do at all.

Mixed vegetable tempura with ponzu dipping sauce

SERVES 4
PREPARATION TIME: 15 MINUTES
COOKING TIME: ABOUT 2 MINUTES

FOR THE PONZU DIPPING SAUCE:

100ml soy sauce

2 tablespoons rice wine vinegar

3cm piece ginger, finely grated

2 tablespoons lime juice

2 tablespoons orange juice

FOR THE TEMPURA BATTER:

2 egg yolks

360ml iced water

2 teaspoons cornflour

200g self-raising flour

FOR THE REST:

1 litre vegetable oil, for deep-frying

12 asparagus spears

12 purple sprouting broccoli spears

6 baby aubergines, halved

1 red pepper, deseeded and sliced

150g mixed oyster and enoki mushrooms, torn if large

Start by mixing all the ingredients together to make the ponzu dipping sauce and set aside.

To make the batter, use chopsticks or a fork to beat the egg yolks and water together. Stir in the flours quickly to keep the batter light and don't worry about any lumps – they won't matter at all.

Pour the oil into a large wok or deep saucepan and heat to 170°C (325°F/Gas 3). If you don't have a thermometer drop a little batter into the pan – it should sizzle immediately if hot enough. Have a large plate lined with absorbent kitchen paper ready. Use chopsticks or tongs to dip the vegetables, one by one, into the batter to coat, then lower straight into the oil. Cook for a minute or 2 until light golden all over. Be careful not to overcrowd the pan or the temperature of the oil will drop; it's better to cook the tempura in batches. Remove with a slotted spoon and drain on the plate lined with absorbent kitchen paper when done.

Serve straight away with dishes of the ponzu dipping sauce.

Small Bites

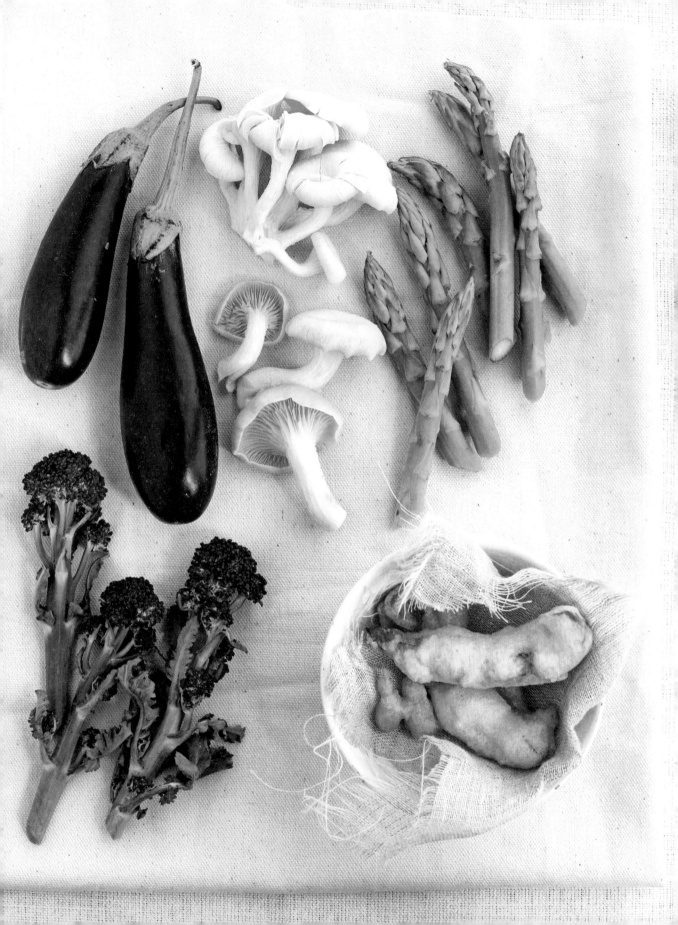

Big Salads

Chapter Three

This is a beautiful and gossamer-fine salad, more suited to a role as a starter than a main course. It's incredibly lovely but not quite substantial enough to call itself a main meal.

Shaved salad with toasted seeds

SERVES 4
PREPARATION TIME: 25 MINUTES

FOR THE DRESSING:

2 tablespoons cider vinegar

75ml tablespoons extra virgin olive oil

1 teaspoon fennel seeds

a small handful of fennel herb, roughly chopped

FOR THE REST:

2 medium beetroot with leaves, scrubbed but not peeled

2 small fennel bulbs, halved

½ forced rhubarb stalk

1 red apple, quartered and cored

2 chicory bulbs, shredded

3 tablespoons mixed seeds, toasted

Start with the dressing: combine all the ingredients and season well.

Trim the leaves from the beetroot and reserve.

Use a mandolin slicer, a sharp knife or even a vegetable peeler to pare the beetroot, fennel bulbs, rhubarb and apple into fine strips or slices. Place in a bowl and add the beetroot leaves and shredded chicory. Toss with the dressing.

Divide between serving plates and scatter each serving with a couple of teaspoons of toasted seeds.

Describing this recipe as a salad might be pushing the definition slightly, but it does contain a dressing and green leaves! Mujadhara, a traditional Middle Eastern dish, is a delicious combination of golden onions, lentils and rice – I use brown basmati for its character.

Warm salad of slow-roast tomatoes, labne and almonds, on mujadhara

SERVES 4
PREPARATION TIME: 20 MINUTES
COOKING TIME: 1 HOUR

FOR THE MUJADHARA:

2 tablespoons olive oil

1 large onion, sliced

250g brown lentils

150g brown basmati rice

FOR THE REST:

a pinch of saffron threads

2 tablespoons sherry vinegar

3 tablespoons olive oil

1 large bunch flat leaf parsley, leaves only

50g baby spinach leaves

12 slow-roast tomato halves
(see page 242)

150g labne (see page 50) or curd cheese

3 tablespoons flaked almonds,
lightly toasted

For the mujadhara, warm the olive oil in a large saucepan, add the sliced onion with a generous pinch of salt and soften over a low heat for 20 minutes. Turn up the heat and fry for 10 minutes more until the onion is deeply golden. Add the lentils and cover with 600ml water. Bring to the boil, cover and simmer gently for 10 minutes. Stir in the rice, re-cover and simmer for 20 minutes more. Remove from the heat and leave to steam for 10 minutes.

Meanwhile, soak the saffron in a couple of tablespoons of boiling water for 5 minutes. Add the vinegar and olive oil to make a dressing and season with salt and pepper.

Combine the parsley (reserving a small handful), spinach and the mujadhara. Pile into a serving bowl and top with the tomatoes, scoops of labne or curd cheese, flaked almonds, the remaining parsley (roughly chopped) and the dressing. Serve warm or at room temperature.

This is a deeply gratifying dish for chilly months – it offers the fresh and lively flavours of a salad, but the comfort of a more substantial meal. Keep an eye on the nuts after adding them to the roast carrots and shallots – they're all too easy to scorch.

A winter salad

SERVES 4
PREPARATION TIME: 20 MINUTES
COOKING TIME: 35 MINUTES

300g small carrots

6 shallots, halved

75ml olive oil

150g walnuts, roughly chopped

150g prunes, stoned and halved

200g faro or spelt

2 tablespoons sherry vinegar

½ garlic clove, crushed

1 teaspoon Dijon mustard

1 small bunch flat leaf parsley, leaves chopped

175g chèvre

Preheat the oven to 190°C (375°F/Gas 5). Halve or thickly slice the carrots depending on their size and toss with the shallots, 2 tablespoons of the olive oil and plenty of salt and pepper. Spread out on a baking tray and roast for about 25 minutes until caramelised and soft. Add the walnuts and prunes to the tray, sprinkling them evenly over the veg, and return to the oven to toast for a further 5–10 minutes.

Meanwhile, cover the faro with 500ml cold water in a saucepan. Add a generous pinch of salt and bring to the boil. Cover and reduce the heat, leaving the faro to simmer merrily for 25 minutes.

When this is done, drain off any remaining water then cover the pan and set the faro aside.

Make the dressing by whisking the remaining olive oil, vinegar, crushed garlic and mustard together with a little salt and pepper. It should be slightly sharp to counter the sweet carrots and prunes. Combine the faro, roast carrot mixture, half the parsley and half the dressing in a serving bowl. Crumble the chèvre over the faro and vegetables, drizzle with the remaining dressing and scatter with the rest of the parsley.

Big Salads

This warm salad bursts with the sweet tastes of North Africa and the extra large couscous grains absorb all the delicious flavours. It's a breeze to make the charmoula dressing recipe on page 244 – this versatile seasoning is always handy to have on standby in the refrigerator.

Giant couscous salad with preserved lemon and charmoula

SERVES 4
PREPARATION TIME: 25 MINUTES
COOKING TIME: 50 MINUTES

500g young parsnips

3 red peppers, deseeded and sliced

3 tablespoons olive oil

2 tablespoons honey

2 preserved lemons, quartered

150g Israeli or giant couscous

1 quantity charmoula dressing
(see page 244)

juice of 1 lemon

1 small bunch coriander, leaves only

200g Greek yoghurt

Preheat the oven to 200°C (400°F/Gas 6). Slice the parsnips lengthways into halves or quarters depending on their size. Place in a roasting tin with the peppers and coat with half the olive oil and honey. Season well and roast for about 35 minutes until caramelised. Slice the flesh from the preserved lemon quarters and discard. Cut the peel into strips.

Heat the remaining olive oil in a large saucepan, add the couscous and stir over a medium heat until golden – this will only take 4 minutes or so. Pour in 200ml boiling water and simmer gently for about 10 minutes until the water has been absorbed and the couscous is tender.

Combine the roasted parsnips and peppers with the couscous, and add 1 tablespoon charmoula, the preserved lemon peel, lemon juice and most of the coriander.

Ripple the remaining charmoula through the yoghurt and serve spooned onto the salad with the rest of the coriander.

 Big Salads

When blood oranges come into season, celebrate them with this salad. The contrasting colours of the snow-white cheese, purple leaves and deep red fruit looks glorious, and tastes it, too. It's best eaten as fresh as possible, so make it at the very last minute.

Blood orange, mozzarella, toasted sourdough and radicchio salad

SERVES 4
PREPARATION TIME: 15 MINUTES
COOKING TIME: 15 MINUTES

3 thick slices sourdough bread

a little olive oil

3 blood oranges

2 tablespoons red wine vinegar

75ml extra virgin olive oil

1 medium head radicchio, trimmed

a handful of wild rocket

2 balls buffalo mozzarella,
torn into pieces

Preheat the oven to 180°C (350°F/Gas 4). Tear the bread into rough pieces – they should be about the size of a small egg – and coat with the olive oil. Spread out on a baking tray and bake for about 15 minutes, shaking and stirring halfway, until golden and crisp. Set aside.

Meanwhile, place the oranges in a shallow dish – you want to catch all the juice – and cut off the tops and bottoms to expose the flesh, then carefully pare the skin away from the sides, following the curve of the fruit. Slice horizontally into discs. Measure 4 tablespoons of the collected juice into a separate bowl, and into this whisk the vinegar and olive oil. Season with salt and pepper.

Tear the radicchio into large pieces and add to the rocket in a large bowl. Throw in the toasted bread, blood oranges and mozzarella. Drizzle with the dressing and toss very gently. Serve straight away.

The choice is yours here: toss all the ingredients together to make a vibrant salad, or if you prefer daintier bites, wrap avocado slices around the addictive pickles to make fun appetisers or canapés.

Salad of avocado, white radish and carrot pickle, and satay dressing

SERVES 4 AS A STARTER
PREPARATION TIME: 25 MINUTES
PLUS PICKLING TIME

FOR THE SALAD OR WRAPS:

1 large carrot

12cm piece white radish (mooli or daikon), peeled

3 tablespoons white wine vinegar

2 tablespoons caster sugar

4 ripe but firm avocados

juice of ½ lime

a small handful of coriander or alfalfa sprouts

FOR THE DRESSING:

1 tablespoon sesame oil

2 tablespoons peanuts, toasted and finely chopped

1 tablespoon soy sauce

1 tablespoon caster sugar

3cm piece ginger, finely chopped

1 red chilli, deseeded and very finely chopped

finely grated juice and zest of 1 lime

To make the pickle, cut the carrot and radishes in half widthways then lengthways, and slice into fine shreds. Place in a non-metallic bowl with the vinegar, sugar and 2 tablespoons water. Cover and set aside for at least 20 minutes or chill for up to 2 days.

Make the dressing by combining all the ingredients in a small bowl.

Halve the avocados and remove the stones. Score the skin from top to bottom with a sharp knife and peel it away carefully. Use a swivel peeler to shave the avocado into long, wide strips. Sprinkle with a little lime juice to prevent them turning brown. Chop any remaining avocado into fine dice.

If you're making a salad, gently toss the salad ingredients together, including the pickle, and spoon a little dressing over to serve. Offer the rest of the dressing alongside.

If you'd rather make little salad wraps, drain the pickle (you can use the liquid to make another batch) and add the coriander or alfalfa sprouts and diced avocado. Lay the avocado slices out flat and place a spoonful of the pickle and salad mixture at one end. Roll up tightly. Spoon the dressing over and serve straight away.

Risoni, a rice-shaped pasta, is what makes this salad work so well. Cook until al dente, then quickly drain and soak with the simple dressing. The hot risoni will absorb the flavours beautifully and be ready to serve straight away. It's also fabulous eaten cold.

Artichoke, risoni and broad bean salad with shaved pecorino

SERVES 4
PREPARATION TIME: 20 MINUTES
COOKING TIME: 25 MINUTES

12 fresh young globe artichokes
or 12 whole marinated artichoke hearts

a few lemon slices and a squeeze of lemon (optional)

350g dried risoni pasta

200g broad beans, podded weight, skins removed

finely grated zest and juice of 1 lemon

4 tablespoons olive oil

4 lemon thyme sprigs, leaves stripped

75g pecorino sardo

If you're going the long way round and using fresh artichokes, fill a bowl with cold water and add a few lemon slices and a squeeze of lemon. This is to stop the trimmed artichokes turning black.

Cut off the tough tops of the artichoke leaves then use a small knife to pare off the tough outer leaves, and remove most of the stalks. Drop each finished artichoke into the bowl of water as you work. When done, drain and transfer to a saucepan, cover with fresh water, add a squeeze of lemon and bring to the boil. Simmer for 25 minutes or so until just tender. Drain, then cut each artichoke heart into quarters. If you're using deli-style marinated artichoke hearts, simply cut each one into quarters.

Bring a large saucepan of water to the boil, add a hefty pinch of salt and tip in the risoni. Cook until al dente, adding the podded and skinned broad beans for the last 2 minutes of cooking. Drain the pasta and beans, transfer to a bowl, and while still warm, dress with the lemon zest, lemon juice, olive oil, lemon thyme and salt and pepper.

Use a vegetable peeler to pare shavings of pecorino over the risoni and verdant broad beans, and gently fold through the artichoke hearts.

Quinoa is not actually a grain, but a member of the beet, spinach and chard family. It is, however, cooked in a very similar way to most other wholegrains. Here it is simmered to tenderness in a mushroom-spiked stock. When cooked, each grain will unfurl like a stretched coil.

Quinoa with parsley pesto, cranberries, toasted hazelnuts and mushrooms

SERVES 4
PREPARATION TIME: 25 MINUTES
COOKING TIME: 25 MINUTES

15g dried mushrooms
(porcini, for example)

30g butter

1 tablespoon olive oil

250g mixed fresh mushrooms,
sliced if large

2 shallots, finely chopped

1 garlic clove, finely chopped

175g quinoa

100g dried cranberries

1 quantity parsley pesto (see page 238)
made with hazelnuts instead of almonds

a squeeze of lemon

75g hazelnuts, toasted and
roughly chopped

Place the dried mushrooms in a heatproof measuring jug and add enough just-boiled water to reach the 350ml mark. Set aside.

Melt half the butter with the olive oil in a deep frying pan. Keep the heat high and fry the mixed fresh mushrooms briskly for a couple of minutes, stirring until they are golden. Tip into a bowl and set aside. Return the pan to a slightly more gentle heat. Add the remaining butter and the shallots to the pan and cook for a few minutes until softened. Add the garlic and quinoa and cook, stirring, for about 5 minutes until the quinoa takes on a pale golden colour.

Strain the soaked mushrooms through a sieve, reserving the water, and roughly chop, then add them to the quinoa. Pour in the strained mushroom water and bring to the boil. Throw in a good pinch of salt, then lower the heat and simmer gently for 18–20 minutes until the quinoa is soft and the liquid is absorbed. Fold in the cranberries and reserved browned mushrooms and set aside.

Stir a couple of tablespoons of pesto through the salad, plus a squeeze of lemon. Spoon a little more pesto over the salad and sprinkle with hazelnuts. Best served warm.

This is guacamole – but not as you know it. In an elegant twist on the traditional dip, this dish is much more of a proper meal than a snack, and sufficient ingredients are included here for four main courses: even the tortilla chips. Feel free, however, to eat it with your fingers.

Guacamole salad

SERVES 4
PREPARATION TIME: 20 MINUTES
PLUS MACERATING TIME
COOKING TIME: ABOUT 15 MINUTES

2 garlic cloves, crushed

finely grated zest and juice of 2 limes

4 tablespoons olive oil

3 wheat flour or corn tortillas

1 small red onion, halved and very finely sliced

1 teaspoon cumin seeds, toasted in a dry pan

3 large avocados, halved and stoned

2 red chicory bulbs

5 spring onions, finely sliced

1 small bunch coriander, leaves only

Preheat the oven to 180°C (350°F/Gas 4). Mix the crushed garlic with the lime zest and olive oil, season with salt and pepper and brush a little of this mixture lightly over both sides of the tortillas. Slice each tortilla into 8 wedges and space out on a baking tray lined with non-stick baking paper. Cook for 12–15 minutes, turning halfway, until crisp and golden. Set aside to cool. The tortilla chips will keep for a few days in an airtight container.

Squeeze the lime juice over the red onion and set aside for 10 minutes to macerate. Add the remaining garlicky oil to the onions and stir in the toasted cumin seeds.

Slice the avocados and combine with the remaining ingredients, including the toasted tortillas, and serve before they soften.

To sprout small seeds like alfalfa or mustard, use 2–3 tablespoons at a time. For the larger mung beans, wheat berries and lentils start with 75g. And for the still larger likes of peas, almonds and chickpeas use about 200g per jar.

How to grow sprouts

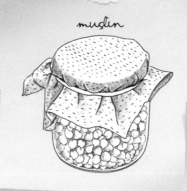

muslin

soak seeds 4–8 hours

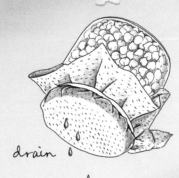

drain

step 1.

Soak your chosen seeds or nuts for 4–8 hours in plenty of cold water. A large, wide glass jar is ideal for this but if you have a specially designed sprouter, follow the instructions on the box.

step 2.

Secure a piece of loose-weave muslin or gauze, or cut-up tights, firmly over the opening of the jar with a rubber band. This will allow the air to circulate; a close-weave material will not 'breathe' and will encourage mould.

step 3.

Invert the jar and drain the water away. The seeds should now be spread out along the inside of the jar.

A wide variety of nuts, seeds and pulses are perfect for sprouting including peas, almonds, mung beans, hazelnuts, chickpeas and sunflower seeds.

rinse

× 2 daily

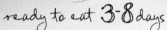

ready to eat 3–8 days

leave 45°

step 5.

Rinse the jar out with clean, cold water twice a day and return it to its angled position with the material or tights re-secured. This will stop the sprouts from growing mouldy.

step 6.

Different nut, seeds and pulses sprout at different times, but shoots will start to grow within a couple of days and the sprouts should be ready to eat in 3–8 days, depending on the variety and how long you want the sprouts to be. Do keep rinsing and swirling them with cold water twice every day to keep them fresh as they grow. Refrigerate finished sprouts whenever you like the look and taste of them. They are now ready to add to salads, juices, soups, sandwiches, hummus or to eat as they are.

step 4.

Prop the jar with the opening facing down at a 45 degree angle, with a bowl or tray underneath to catch any water that drips out. Leave in a cool place, out of direct sunlight.

Cherry tomatoes come in a rainbow of colours and a range of shapes and sizes: orange, yellow, black, red, round, oval and teardrop. A selection looks stunning atop this verdant tabbouleh.

Green tabbouleh topped with a cherry tomato salad

SERVES 4
PREP TIME: 15 MINUTES
PLUS SOAKING TIME

150g bulgur wheat

2 large bunches flat leaf parsley, leaves only

1 large bunch mint, leaves only

½ cucumber, peeled, deseeded and very finely diced

1 bunch spring onions, finely sliced

juice of 2 lemons

75ml olive oil

300g cherry tomatoes, halved if large

Cover the bulgur wheat generously with warm water and leave to soak for 1 hour. Drain well, squeezing the excess water out. Finely chop the parsley and mint leaves – they should be chopped very small – and mix with the soaked and drained wheat. Add the diced cucumber. Stir well and then add most of the spring onions, keeping some back for the tomato salad.

Combine the lemon juice and olive oil and season well with salt and pepper to make a dressing. Pour most of it over the wheat mixture. Taste and adjust the seasoning as needed, then spoon onto a serving plate. Top with the cherry tomatoes, a scattering of the remaining spring onions and the rest of the dressing.

When asparagus season comes around, the air can still be distinctly chilly – and chilly days call for warm, substantial salads. Here, the gently chewy barley grains mop up the wonderful flavours of the dressing.

Griddled asparagus and warm pearl barley salad with chive dressing

SERVES 4
PREPARATION TIME: 20 MINUTES
COOKING TIME: 50 MINUTES

2 tablespoons olive oil

1 leek, thinly sliced

225g pearl barley

520ml vegetable stock

1 x 400g tin haricot beans, drained

250g asparagus, woody ends trimmed

FOR THE DRESSING:

juice of 2 lemons

1 egg yolk

75ml olive oil

a small bunch of chives, finely chopped, plus whole stalks, to serve (optional)

Heat a tablespoon of olive oil in a large saucepan and add the sliced leek. Cook gently for 5 minutes, stirring, until softened but not coloured. Add the pearl barley followed by the stock and bring to the boil. Reduce the heat so that the liquid simmers gently and leave it to cook for about 40 minutes, or until nearly all the liquid is absorbed. The barley should be tender with a bit of bite. Stir in the drained haricot beans and cook for a further 5 minutes to heat them through. Cover with a lid and set aside.

While the barley cooks, make the dressing. Whisk the lemon juice and egg yolk together in a bowl with a pinch of salt. As you continue whisking, gradually pour in the olive oil, drop by drop at first, to form a thick, creamy dressing. Stir in half the chopped chives and season to taste.

Place a griddle pan over a high heat. Coat the asparagus in the remaining tablespoon of olive oil and season well with salt and pepper. When the pan is smoking hot, spread the asparagus spears out in a single layer and griddle them for 2–3 minutes, turning until blackened on all sides.

Serve the pearl barley in warmed bowls and top with the griddled asparagus, the dressing, the remaining chopped chives and whole chive stalks (if using).

The contrasting toppings of this spiced, Indian-style salad sing with crisp pomegranate seeds and luscious yoghurt. Texture is just as important as wonderful flavour and vibrant colour in this dish.

Chana chaat

SERVES 4
PREPARATION TIME: 25 MINUTES
COOKING TIME: 25 MINUTES

FOR THE CHICKPEAS:

1 small onion, halved and sliced

2cm piece ginger, finely grated

1 green chilli, deseeded and finely chopped

2 tablespoons groundnut oil

300g cooked chickpeas, or 1 x 400g tin, drained

½ teaspoon mild chilli powder

1 teaspoon garam masala

FOR THE REST:

½ cucumber, peeled, deseeded and diced

2 vine tomatoes, diced

a squeeze of lemon

1 small bunch coriander, roughly chopped, plus extra leaves, to serve

4 heaped tablespoons natural yoghurt

seeds from 1 pomegranate

2 large cooked poppadoms, roughly crushed

Sauté the onion, ginger and chilli in the oil for 5 minutes until the onion is soft. Add the chickpeas and cook for a further 5 minutes until golden. Now add the chilli powder and garam masala and cook for 2 minutes more. Remove from the heat, season well and set aside to cool.

Mix the cucumber, tomatoes, lemon juice and the chopped coriander in a mixing bowl. Divide between 4 plates and top with the chickpea mixture, yoghurt, pomegranate seeds and the crushed poppadoms.

Sprinkle with the coriander leaves and serve before the poppadoms soften.

Big Salads

Choose a really ripe Camembert or Brie for this salad and the most luscious black figs you can lay your hands on, and you have the perfect partnership here. You could use the pickled fruit recipe on page 244 instead of the cooked figs if you prefer.

Camembert, watercress and marinated figs with walnut dressing

SERVES 4
PREPARATION TIME: 25 MINUTES
PLUS MARINATING TIME
COOKING TIME: 10 MINUTES

200ml balsamic vinegar

100g caster sugar

2 garlic cloves, bruised

6 thyme sprigs

6 plump figs, halved

4 tablespoons walnut oil

a large handful of watercress, thick stalks trimmed

150g ripe Camembert or Brie, sliced

75g walnuts, toasted and roughly chopped

Place the vinegar, sugar, garlic and 4 of the thyme sprigs in a saucepan and add 100ml water. Bring to the boil and simmer for a minute to dissolve the sugar and cook out some of the vinegary flavour. Set aside to cool for 5 minutes then pour over the halved figs and leave to marinate for an hour or two.

Discard the thyme sprigs and garlic from the marinade and spoon 5 tablespoons into a small lidded jar. Strip the leaves from the remaining 2 thyme sprigs and add to the jar with the walnut oil, a little salt and plenty of pepper. Screw on the lid and shake well until combined to make a dressing.

Heat a non-stick frying pan over a medium-high heat and sear the drained figs, cut sides down, for a minute or so until they caramelise. Remove the pan from the heat, turn the figs over and set aside.

In a large bowl, drizzle the watercress with a little of the dressing, tossing to coat the leaves. Add the Camembert or Brie, walnuts and caramelised figs and divide between serving plates. Spoon the remaining dressing over each plate of salad.

Griddled lettuce: I know it sounds odd, but have faith. Lightly charred lettuce is an underrated beast and makes a very special Caesar salad. Be careful not to overcook the leaves as they will lose their colour and vibrancy – limp leaves are not what you want here.

Grilled Caesar salad

SERVES 4
PREPARATION TIME: 15 MINUTES
COOKING TIME: 10 MINUTES

1 garlic clove, crushed

100ml olive oil

6 Little Gem lettuces, halved lengthways

1 egg yolk

1 teaspoon Dijon mustard

60g Parmesan

juice of ½ lemon

4 long, thin baguette slices

a handful of chopped flat leaf parsley, to serve

Combine the garlic with the olive oil and brush a little over the lettuce halves. Season with salt and pepper.

Whisk the egg yolk in a bowl with the mustard and a tablespoon of finely grated Parmesan. As you continue whisking, very slowly pour in the remaining olive oil and garlic mixture until a thick dressing forms. Add the lemon juice and a tablespoon of water to thin the consistency a little.

Place a griddle pan over a high heat. Sear the lettuce, cut sides down first, until they begin to char – this will take about 2 minutes. Turn over and griddle for a further 2 minutes or so. Finely grate enough Parmesan over the lettuce to lightly coat. Divide between serving plates.

Preheat the grill to medium and toast the baguette slices for a few minutes until golden on both sides. Spread a little dressing over one side and perch next to the lettuce. Drizzle the rest of the dressing over the salad, sprinkle with parsley and a few Parmesan shavings.

Salad toppings

2
Toasted garlic breadcrumbs

Warm about 3 tablespoons fruity olive oil in a large frying pan with 2 crushed garlic cloves and cook over a very low heat for a few minutes. Add a cupful of stale ciabatta or sourdough breadcrumbs. Stir over a medium heat for a few minutes until browned and toasted, then set aside to cool.

1
Maple walnuts

Coat 100g walnuts with 2 tablespoons maple syrup, 1 tablespoon finely chopped rosemary and a pinch of cayenne pepper. Season well. Spread on a baking tray lined with non-stick baking paper. Cook at 160°C (315°F/Gas 2–3) for 15 minutes, stirring halfway, until golden. Cool before roughly chopping.

Tahini seeds

Spread 200g mixed seeds on a large baking tray and roast at 180°C (350°F/Gas 4) for 5 minutes. Combine 2 tablespoons light tahini paste, 1 tablespoon runny honey, ½ a crushed garlic clove and 1 tablespoon sesame oil in a large bowl. Tip in the hot seeds and mix well. Spread out on the baking tray again and bake for another 5 minutes. Set aside to cool then crumble over salads as needed.

3

Take Six

4
Olive and polenta cubes

Stir 250g quick-cook polenta in 1 litre simmering veg stock for 3 minutes until thick. Add 1 large handful grated Parmesan and 4 tablespoons finely chopped olives. Season well. Spread on a tray to a thickness of about 2.5cm and cool. Once firm, cut the polenta into 2.5cm cubes and sauté in olive oil until browned.

6
Roast, spiced chickpeas

Thoroughly drain 800g chickpeas (freshly cooked or tinned) then toss with 1 tablespoon olive oil, a pinch of cayenne, 1 teaspoon ground cumin and 1 teaspoon ground coriander. Spread out on a baking tray lined with non-stick baking paper. Cook for about 45 minutes at 180°C (350°F/Gas 4) until crisp and golden, shaking the tray every now and then to redistribute the chickpeas.

5
Crisp Parmesan lace

Line a large baking tray with non-stick baking paper. Drop mounds of finely grated Parmesan on the tray at regular intervals (the cheese will spread out as it cooks) and bake at 200°C (400°F/Gas 6) for 3–4 minutes until golden and bubbling. Leave the cheese to settle for a minute then remove with a spatula and leave to cool. Scatter over salads as they are, or break into pieces.

Soups

Chapter Four

This is for days when you can't bring yourself to switch the oven on, because there's no cooking involved at all. The only potential hitch is that you'll need a juicer instead! It's a very satisfying dish, as the ripe avocado adds body and richness to all that raw vegetable virtue.

Raw vegetable and avocado soup

SERVES 4
PREPARATION TIME: 10 MINUTES

3 large carrots

50g spinach leaves

4 celery sticks

3cm piece fresh ginger

2 large, very ripe avocados, halved and stoned

iced water

juice of ½ lime

1 tablespoon soy sauce

2–3 drops Tabasco sauce

ice cubes, toasted sesame oil and coriander leaves, to serve

Pass the carrots, spinach, celery and ginger through a juicer and then transfer the juice to a blender. Blitz with the avocados until smooth. Make the quantity up to 800ml with iced water, lime juice, soy and Tabasco. Blend again.

Serve with ice cubes, a drop or 2 of sesame oil and some perky coriander leaves to serve.

Soups

A vegetarian hot and sour soup is less complex than its fish or meat-based counterparts, but what it loses in depth it gains in freshness and clarity. Vegetarian versions of fish sauce are readily available, but a little soy will do nicely instead. Serve this as a starter, part of a Southeast Asian meal or a stand-alone soup.

Vietnamese hot and sour soup

SERVES 4–8
PREPARATION TIME: 20 MINUTES
COOKING TIME: 15 MINUTES

1 tablespoon groundnut oil

2 shallots, finely sliced

2 lemongrass stalks, bruised
with a rolling pin

2 garlic cloves, finely chopped

2 tablespoons sieved tamarind
pulp or tamarind purée

2 tablespoons caster sugar

750ml vegetable stock (see page 236)
or quality bought stock

2 celery sticks, sliced

2 tomatoes, cored and sliced
into 8 pieces

200g peeled and cored fresh pineapple,
cut into cubes

125g okra, thickly sliced

100g bean sprouts

2 tablespoons vegetarian
fish sauce or soy sauce

a small handful of coriander,
roughly chopped

a small handful of ngo om
(rice paddy herb) or Thai basil leaves

Heat the groundnut oil in a large saucepan and add the shallots, lemongrass, garlic, tamarind pulp or purée and sugar. Soften over a lowish heat for 5 minutes – you don't want the veg to colour. Now add the vegetable stock and simmer for 5 minutes.

Throw in the celery, tomatoes, pineapple and okra, and simmer for another few minutes. Add the bean sprouts and simmer for 5 minutes more. Shake in the vegetarian fish sauce or soy and taste the soup – you might want to add more tamarind, fish sauce, soy sauce or sugar to balance the sweet and the sour.

Lastly, stir in the herbs and serve in small warmed bowls.

Soups

For some reason, lovage is a much underused culinary herb and this chilled soup is a lovely way to discover its virtues. It is simplicity itself to make, as there's no real cooking involved. If lovage leaves are not forthcoming, celery leaves make a perfectly fine substitute.

Chilled cucumber and lovage soup

SERVES 4
PREPARATION TIME: 15 MINUTES

2 cucumbers, peeled and roughly sliced

200ml crème fraîche

200ml natural yoghurt

1 tablespoon chopped lovage leaves

ice cubes and lovage leaves (optional), to serve

Place the cucumbers, 180ml of the crème fraîche, yoghurt and lovage leaves in a blender and liquidise until smooth. Season with salt and pepper to taste. Chill for a few hours.

Serve the chilled soup with teaspoonfuls of the remaining crème fraîche and ice cubes. If you wish, you could add a few lovage leaves to the bowls before serving.

This soup should taste of sunshine, so the ripest and freshest vegetables you can find will be needed to do it justice. If you want to gild the lily further, some good black olives, stoned and diced, and a few oregano leaves are lovely when added to the vegetable garnish.

Gazpacho Andaluz

SERVES 4
PREPARATION TIME: 20 MINUTES
PLUS CHILLING TIME

700g vine-ripened tomatoes

2 red peppers, halved and deseeded

1 large cucumber

1 garlic clove, crushed

½ loaf ciabatta, torn

4 tablespoons sherry vinegar

100ml extra virgin olive oil

2 teaspoons caster sugar

Tabasco sauce, to serve (optional)

ice cubes and basil leaves, to serve

Set aside 2 tomatoes, half a red pepper and a quarter of the cucumber.

Roughly chop the remaining tomatoes, peppers and cucumber and place in a blender with the garlic and bread. Blend to a rough purée. Remove to a bowl, stir in the vinegar and 200ml water and season to taste with salt and pepper. Cover and chill for at least 2 hours or overnight. The bread will swell up and the flavours will mellow.

Before serving, nick the bases of the reserved tomatoes, place in a heatproof bowl and cover with boiling water. Drain the tomatoes and peel the skin away. Chop into fine dice, along with the reserved red pepper and cucumber.

Stir the olive oil into the soup and taste again. Add the sugar, Tabasco sauce (if using) or a little more vinegar, salt or pepper, and even a little extra chilled water to adjust the consistency. The soup should have quite a kick to it so make sure it's good and punchy.

Divide between cold bowls and serve with the ice cubes, a scattering of the diced vegetables and basil leaves.

This list of ingredients rather bossily demands that you peel the green grapes. If the idea horrifies you or there simply aren't enough hours in your day, unpeeled grapes really won't be the end of the world. Whichever way you go, this unusual and subtle soup is wonderful.

White gazpacho

SERVES 4
PREPARATION TIME: 20 MINUTES
PLUS SOAKING AND CHILLING TIME

150g country-style bread (sourdough, for example)

250ml milk

2 garlic cloves, finely chopped

75g blanched almonds

175ml extra virgin olive oil

2 tablespoons sherry vinegar

150g green grapes, peeled and halved

25g blanched almonds

In a bowl, cover the bread with the milk and set aside for 20 minutes.

Place the soaked bread in a food processor with the garlic, blanched almonds and a pinch of salt, then process until a purée forms.

Slowly add the olive oil in a steady stream while the motor is still running. Scrape into a bowl and stir in the vinegar with 420ml cold water and salt and pepper to taste.

Cover and chill for at least 2 hours or overnight. Divide between chilled bowls and sprinkle with the grapes and blanched almonds.

The smoky depth of this soup comes from the magic chipotle pepper. You can buy it dried – in which case it will need soaking – or in jars. This will only get better if you have the chance to make it a day or two ahead.

Smoky black bean and roast tomato soup

SERVES 4
PREPARATION TIME: 20 MINUTES
COOKING TIME: 55 MINUTES

FOR THE SALSA:

1 small red onion, very finely chopped

1 tablespoon sunflower oil

100g sweetcorn kernels

1 red chilli, deseeded and finely chopped

a squeeze of lime

1 small bunch coriander, leaves only

FOR THE SOUP:

1 tablespoon sunflower oil

2 red onions, chopped

3 garlic cloves, finely chopped

2 teaspoons chipotle pepper paste

1 teaspoon fresh or dried oregano

1 tablespoon cumin seeds

12 roast tomato halves

700g cooked black beans

750ml vegetable stock (see page 236) or quality bought stock

a squeeze of lime

sour cream, to serve

Start with the salsa. Cook the red onion in the sunflower oil for 5 minutes until soft and beginning to colour. Turn up the heat and add the sweetcorn and chilli, stirring until the corn is toasted at the edges. Remove from the heat, season with salt and pepper and add a squeeze of lime.

To make the soup, heat the oil in a large saucepan, add the onions and sauté slowly until translucent but not coloured. Add the garlic, chipotle pepper or paste, oregano and cumin seeds. Continue to cook for a further 5 minutes until the cumin is fragrant.

Add the roast tomato halves, cooked beans and vegetable stock, and bring to the boil. Simmer for 30 minutes. Season with salt, pepper and lime juice then liquidise in a blender until smooth. Check the seasoning and adjust if needed.

Stir the coriander into the salsa.

Ladle the soup into warmed bowls and top with a spoonful of sour cream and a spoonful of salsa.

There might be a lot of chopping here, but this recipe is child's play and the result is special enough to warrant the extra effort. The cream adds a certain silky richness but can be left out without any ill-effects. This is lovely served cool the next day – the vegetables may not be as sprightly but will have gained wisdom and character.

Summer minestrone

SERVES 4
PREPARATION TIME: 15 MINUTES
COOKING TIME: 45 MINUTES

2 tablespoons olive oil

2 garlic cloves, finely chopped

2 shallots, finely chopped

2 celery sticks, finely chopped

1 fennel bulb, finely chopped

200g young broad beans, podded weight, skins removed

200g young fresh peas, podded weight

150g green beans, sliced

250g asparagus tips, sliced

950ml vegetable stock (see page 236) or quality bought stock

a handful each of mint and basil leaves

75ml double cream

4 tablespoons fresh pesto (see page 238), to serve

Heat the olive oil in a large saucepan and soften the garlic, shallots, celery and fennel. It should take about 10 minutes.

Add half the broad beans, peas, green beans and asparagus. Cook, stirring, for 5 minutes. Pour in the stock, bring to the boil and simmer for about 25 minutes.

Add the other half of the vegetables to the saucepan and cook for 5 minutes more. Remove from the heat and pour in a little extra boiling water if the soup appears too thick for your liking. Add the herbs and cream and season to taste.

Ladle into warmed bowls and drop a spoonful of pesto into each to serve.

Soups

The humble potato has been ruthlessly fired from chowder duty and replaced with the more vivacious butternut squash, cubes of which dot this pale soup like orange jewels. But either vegetable works well in this dish, so don't hesitate to reinstate potato if you have some to hand – 500g will do nicely – to produce a slightly milder soup.

Winter squash and corn chowder

SERVES 4
PREPARATION TIME: 20 MINUTES
COOKING TIME: 25 MINUTES

1 small butternut squash

40g butter

1 small onion, finely chopped

1 fennel bulb, finely chopped

1 carrot, finely chopped

1 garlic clove, finely chopped

½ teaspoon dried chilli flakes

2 tablespoons plain flour

700ml vegetable stock (see page 236) or quality bought stock

200ml full fat milk

2 sweetcorn cobs, kernels sliced off

a small bunch of dill, finely chopped

a squeeze of lime, to taste

Peel the butternut squash with a swivel vegetable peeler. Cut in half lengthways, scoop out the seeds and dice the flesh into large cubes.

Melt the butter in a large, deep saucepan. Add the onion, fennel, carrot and garlic, and cook gently for 10 minutes, stirring often, until softened but not coloured. Add the chilli flakes and flour and stir for a further minute, followed by the cubed squash and vegetable stock. Bring to the boil and simmer for 10 minutes or so until the squash is tender.

Add the milk, sweetcorn and dill and simmer for 5 minutes more. Season well and add a squeeze of lime.

Soups

Sometimes a rich main course demands a very light starter to get the ball rolling, and this fits the bill very prettily: a clear, ruby broth that will tempt but not overstuff your eager diners. Do try to avoid the beetroot that's ready-cooked, vinegared and wrapped in plastic – what you want is the fresh stuff full of all that sweet, earthy flavour.

Beetroot and porcini broth

SERVES 4
PREPARATION TIME: 10 MINUTES
COOKING TIME: 30 MINUTES
PLUS STEEPING TIME

20g dried porcini

3 large beetroot, peeled and roughly chopped

2 carrots, roughly chopped

1 celery stick, roughly chopped

a handful of chervil including stalks, plus extra sprigs to garnish

TO SEASON:

a squeeze of lemon

1 teaspoon caster sugar

Place all the ingredients in a large saucepan with 800ml water. Bring to the boil very slowly and simmer gently for 30 minutes. Remove from the heat and leave to stand for 20 minutes then strain through a fine sieve. Reserve the mushrooms and one of the beetroot.

Finely dice the porcini and the reserved beetroot and add to the strained broth. Season with the lemon juice, sugar and some salt and pepper.

Divide between bowls and garnish with chervil sprigs.

Soups

Celeriac soup is heavenly and loves being made in advance –
perhaps the night before you plan to eat it – to give the ingredients
time to get to know each other. The soup will then be ready to be
reheated and served hot, or it works extremely well eaten chilled.

Butter bean and celeriac velouté with charmoula

SERVES 4
PREPARATION TIME: 20 MINUTES
COOKING TIME: 35 MINUTES

1 celeriac, about 500g, cubed

a squeeze of lemon

2 celery sticks, finely chopped

1 onion, finely chopped

2 garlic cloves, chopped

2 tablespoons olive oil

300g cooked butter beans

½ teaspoon salt

2 tablespoons crème fraîche (optional)

4 tablespoons charmoula dressing
(see page 244)

Drop the cubed celeriac into a bowl of cold water with a squeeze of lemon. This will stop it browning.

Cook the celery, onion and garlic in the olive oil for 10 minutes until soft and translucent but not brown. Add the celeriac and cook for a further 5 minutes, then tip the butter beans in with 800ml water and the salt. Bring to the boil and simmer for about 20 minutes.

Liquidise in a blender with the crème fraîche (if using) until completely smooth. For a truly velvety soup, push the mixture through a sieve. Adjust the seasoning. Serve chilled or reheat gently until piping hot. Add a spoonful of charmoula dressing to each serving.

Soups

Bread

Chapter Five

You can use all plain white flour in this recipe to make it a bit more refined, or half rye or spelt flour to increase the nutty overtones. The dough might look sticky and shaggy when all the ingredients are mixed together, but don't worry – it's meant to look that way. And remember that a light hand really does produce a light soda bread.

Quick soda bread

MAKES 1 LARGE LOAF
PREPARATION TIME: 15 MINUTES
COOKING TIME: 45 MINUTES

250g plain flour

250g wholemeal plain flour

1 tablespoon caster sugar

1 teaspoon bicarbonate of soda

1 teaspoon salt

30g chilled butter, cubed

650ml buttermilk

Preheat the oven to 200°C (400°F/Gas 6) and line a baking tray with non-stick baking paper.

Sift the flours into a mixing bowl and add back in all the bran you catch in the sieve except for 1 tablespoon, which you need to reserve for later. Stir in the sugar, bicarbonate of soda and salt. Rub in the butter with your fingertips.

Quickly stir in the buttermilk and mix with a palette knife to form a rough dough. Don't overwork the mixture or it will be tough, and work quickly as you form the dough into a round loaf. Sit the dough on the lined baking tray and make a deep cross in the top with a sharp knife. Sprinkle with the reserved tablespoon of bran and bake for about 45 minutes until golden and hollow-sounding when tapped underneath.

Cool on a wire rack, covering with a clean tea towel if you prefer the crust to soften slightly.

This pizza-style rolled up bread is a deliciously easy solution when famished crowds descend. Stromboli freeze incredibly well, so pop one loaf in the freezer and defrost when needed: just heat through in a warm oven and it will be nearly as good as the day it was made.

Olive Stromboli

MAKES 2 LARGE LOAVES
PREPARATION TIME: 30 MINUTES
PLUS RESTING TIME
COOKING TIME: 30 MINUTES

1 teaspoon caster sugar

1 tablespoon fast-action dried yeast

740ml lukewarm water

800g strong white bread flour, plus extra for dusting

1 tablespoon salt

2 tablespoons cornmeal or polenta, for dusting

extra virgin olive oil, for oiling and drizzling

FOR THE FILLING:

a large handful of basil leaves

20 black olives, pitted

150g grilled peppers in olive oil, drained

1 ball buffalo mozzarella, torn into pieces

In a large bowl, mix the sugar, yeast and lukewarm water and set aside for 10 minutes to 'sponge', or begin the fermentation process. Add half the flour and mix well with a spoon. Set aside in a warm place for another 15 minutes.

Now add the salt and remaining flour, then mix to form rough dough – use a wooden spoon at first and when the dough becomes difficult to stir use your hands instead. Turn onto a lightly floured surface and knead for at least 10 minutes (or 5 minutes in a machine with a dough hook) until smooth and elastic. The dough will be very sticky at first but don't be tempted to add extra flour; its stickiness makes the finished loaf light. Turn the dough into an oiled bowl, cover with a damp, clean tea towel and leave in a warm place (an airing cupboard is good) for an hour or until doubled in size.

Preheat the oven to 200°C (400°F/Gas 6) and dust a large, oiled baking tray with a little cornmeal or polenta.

When ready, knock the dough back with a punch. Divide in half and roll or stretch each piece out on a floured surface to form a large rectangle about 20 x 30cm. Scatter half the basil leaves, olives, peppers and mozzarella over the surface and drizzle with a little olive oil. You now need to roll the Stromboli up. With the dough placed long side towards you, gently roll each piece of dough and its filling into a long log shape.

Cover the Stromboli with a damp, clean tea towel and set aside for 15 minutes. Drizzle with olive oil, scatter with a little sea salt and bake for 30 minutes or so until golden and risen. Cool on a wire rack for at least 10 minutes before slicing.

Let no-one tell you that making your own bread requires some kind of talent or special culinary gift. With a little patience (the resting time is long, but it gives this bread its lovely flavour) a chewy and characterful sourdough will be yours with barely a knead.

No-knead sourdough loaf

MAKES 1 LOAF
PREPARATION TIME: 15 MINUTES
PLUS RESTING TIME
COOKING TIME: ABOUT 45 MINUTES

250g strong wholemeal bread flour, plus extra for dusting

250g strong white bread flour

¼ teaspoon fast-action yeast

1½ teaspoons salt

375ml warm water

sunflower oil, for oiling

Combine all the dry ingredients in a large bowl and add the water, stirring with a wooden spoon and then with your hands, to form very soft, sticky dough. It will look 'shaggy' but you don't need to over-mix it. Cover the bowl with clingfilm and leave in a warm place for 15–18 hours.

Lightly flour a work surface and flour your hands – just a little is needed. Fold the dough over on itself, cover with oiled clingfilm and leave for 15 minutes.

Again using minimal flour on your hands and work surface, shape the dough into a ball and slide it onto a sheet of baking paper sprinkled with wholemeal flour. Cover with a clean tea towel and leave for 2 hours until doubled in size.

Before the dough has finished rising, place a large, lidded casserole in the oven and preheat to 220°C (425°F/Gas 7). When the oven is ready, carefully take the hot casserole out, place the dough inside, and replace the lid. Return to the oven for 30 minutes then remove the lid and cook for a further 15 minutes or so until the bread is golden on top. Tip out of the casserole and cool on a wire rack.

Think of this as an extraordinary flatbread rather than your usual pizza. It's rolled out slightly thicker than conventional pizza dough and comes out soft and airy in the middle. Don't be fooled by the simple ingredients: it's a heavenly combination and, served straight from the oven, goes beautifully with soups, salads, dips or roast vegetables.

Pizza Bianca

MAKES 4
PREPARATION TIME: 15 MINUTES
PLUS RESTING TIME
COOKING TIME: 5–10 MINUTES PER PIZZA

250g plain flour

250g strong white bread flour

1 teaspoon fast-action dried yeast

2 teaspoons salt

320ml warm water

4 tablespoons extra virgin olive oil

cornmeal or polenta, for dusting

rosemary leaves and sea salt,
to scatter over

Combine the flours, yeast, salt and warm water in an electric mixer or mixing bowl to form dough. Add a tablespoon of the olive oil. Use a dough hook to knead for 5–8 minutes, or turn onto a lightly floured surface and knead by hand for 10 minutes until the dough is smooth and elastic. Place in an oiled bowl, cover with clingfilm and leave to rest in a warm place for an hour.

Preheat the oven to 230°C (450°F/Gas 8) and if you own a pizza stone or heatproof tile that will fit inside the oven, now is the time to put it in to heat.

Knock back the dough with a punch. Roll out a quarter of the dough on a floured surface (don't use lots of flour) until it forms a circle about 1cm thick. Dust a baking tray with cornmeal or polenta and lay the pizza on it. Drizzle with olive oil and scatter with rosemary and sea salt. Carefully put the tray in the oven – onto the hot pizza stone or tile (if using) – and cook for a few minutes. The timing will very much depend on your oven but it shouldn't be more than 8–10 minutes. While this one's cooking, prepare the next pizza and bake each one in quick succession. Serve each cooked pizza hot and straight out of the oven.

Like the soda bread recipe on page 130, this recipe is also quick, so you won't find any yeast here. It's an ideal mixture to experiment with: you can bake it as a whole loaf or vary the herbs and the root vegetables as you wish. This bread is forgiving and versatile but always best served warm, preferably with a bowl of hot soup.

Parsnip and rosemary rolls

MAKES 6
PREPARATION TIME: 15 MINUTES
COOKING TIME: 25 MINUTES

olive oil, to oil and drizzle

220g parsnips, coarsely grated

275g self-raising flour

1 tablespoon chopped rosemary, plus extra sprigs

1 teaspoon salt

2 eggs, beaten

2 tablespoons milk

Preheat the oven to 190°C (375°F/Gas 5). Oil a baking tray or line it with non-stick baking paper.

Mix the parsnips, flour, rosemary and salt in a large bowl. Make a well in the centre and add the beaten eggs and milk. Use a knife to quickly mix everything together to form rough dough, being careful not to overwork it. Divide the dough into 6 pieces and shape each into a round. Slash the tops with a sharp knife and press a small rosemary sprig onto each. Drizzle with olive oil.

Bake for about 25–30 minutes until golden. Cool on a wire rack if you like, but these rolls are best eaten warm.

Fast

Chapter Six

This makes a complete supper; it's well-balanced and quick, quick, quick. Tempeh is tofu's often overlooked cousin made from fermented soybeans. Alternatively, you could use firm tofu here instead, and the Indian cottage cheese, paneer, would work too.

Tamarind tempeh with sesame noodles and shredded greens

SERVES 2
PREPARATION TIME: 15 MINUTES
PLUS MARINATING TIME
COOKING TIME: 10 MINUTES

250g tempeh, sliced 2cm thick

4cm piece ginger, finely chopped

finely grated zest and juice of
1 small orange

2 tablespoons mild honey

2 tablespoons tamarind paste or purée

2 tablespoons soy sauce,
plus extra to serve

125g medium egg noodles

a little toasted sesame oil

2 tablespoons groundnut oil

1 green chilli, deseeded and
finely chopped

1 garlic clove, finely chopped

150g Asian greens, shredded

2 teaspoons gomashio (see page 236)

2 spring onions, finely shredded

Coat the sliced tempeh with a mixture of half the chopped ginger, the orange zest, honey, tamarind and 1 tablespoon soy sauce. Ideally, leave to marinate for 10–30 minutes.

Cook the noodles according to pack instructions, refresh under cold water and drain. Toss with a very little sesame oil to prevent sticking and set aside. Heat 1 tablespoon groundnut oil in a large wok or frying pan and when it is almost smoking add the tempeh and stir-fry for a few minutes, or until browned on all sides. Remove to a plate.

Pour thẽ remaining groundnut oil into the pan and add the rest of the ginger, chilli and garlic. Cook and stir for a minute, then add the greens. Return the tempeh to the wok or pan and add the orange juice, then toss through over the heat until the greens wilt.

Now add the drained noodles and toss. Divide between 2 warmed bowls and dot with a few drops of sesame oil. Sprinkle with gomashio and finish with the spring onion shreds. Offer more soy sauce at the table.

This raw carpaccio is so pretty and can be ready in a jiffy. Some soft cheese spooned or crumbled over the sliced vegetables will make it a little more sustaining. However, you might prefer to let the dressing sing through on its own for a wonderfully light lunch or supper.

Summer vegetable carpaccio with horseradish dressing

SERVES 2
PREPARATION TIME: 15 MINUTES

2 ripe but firm baby avocados, halved and stoned

juice of ½ lemon

2 radishes, with leaves, scrubbed

3 baby carrots

2 baby courgettes

6cm piece cucumber, peeled, halved and deseeded

1 tablespoon extra virgin olive oil

3 tablespoons horseradish dressing (see page 238)

1 tablespoon cress or pea shoots

Peel the avocados, scoring the skin lengthways first. Use a very sharp knife to shave the flesh into long slices and toss with a little of the lemon juice to prevent browning.

Slice the radishes (set aside the leaves), carrots and courgettes lengthways and pare the cucumber into ribbons with a vegetable peeler. Toss with the radish leaves and the remaining lemon juice and add to the avocados along with the olive oil. Season to taste and arrange on 2 plates. Spoon the horseradish dressing over and scatter with the cress or pea shoots.

This is a pretty but complex little number: by turns salty, crisp, hot, sour, yielding and sweet. It will serve three as a swift starter or two as a summery supper. Make the preparation even quicker by mixing the dressing in advance, so you have it ready in the refrigerator.

Carrot and coriander fritters with halloumi and sweet lemon dressing

SERVES 2–3
PREPARATION TIME: 15 MINUTES
PLUS CHILLING TIME
COOKING TIME: ABOUT 10 MINUTES

FOR THE FRITTERS:

250g halloumi

4 large carrots, coarsely grated or shredded

5 spring onions, finely sliced

a small bunch of coriander, leaves chopped

1 tablespoon coriander seeds, toasted and crushed

20g gram or chickpea flour (or plain flour)

2 eggs, beaten

TO FINISH:

3 tablespoons olive oil

a handful of rocket leaves

4 tablespoons sweet lemon dressing (see page 238)

Coarsely grate 50g of the halloumi and add to the carrots in a mixing bowl. Slice the remaining halloumi and set aside. Add the remaining fritter ingredients to the mixing bowl, season with pepper and just a little salt and mix well. Form into 12 round cakes, flattening them with your hand, and lay out on a tray. If you have time, chill for 30 minutes to firm them up.

Heat the olive oil in a pan and fry the cakes for a couple of minutes on each side until golden. Remove to a plate and keep warm in a low oven while you fry the halloumi for a minute or 2 on each side. You won't need any extra oil for this. When done, the cakes should be crisp and golden.

Layer the fritters and halloumi slices on serving plates with the rocket, and drizzle with the sweet lemon dressing.

These aubergines are happy to be a light and summery supper option when you'd rather not spend much time in the kitchen. Make sure the aubergine is cooked to buttery tenderness before covering with the miso mixture, and it will be sublime. If you love the taste of sesame, include a few drops of sesame oil in the miso topping.

Japanese aubergines with miso

SERVES 4
PREPARATION TIME: 15 MINUTES
COOKING TIME: 6–8 MINUTES

2 tablespoons white miso paste

2 tablespoons caster sugar

1 tablespoon mirin

1 tablespoon rice wine vinegar

4 Japanese aubergines or baby aubergines

2 tablespoons groundnut oil

2 spring onions, finely shredded

2 tablespoons cress, ideally shiso or coriander

2 teaspoons sesame seeds, lightly toasted

steamed rice and pickled (sushi) ginger, to serve

Combine the miso, sugar, mirin and rice wine vinegar, stirring until smooth. Cut the aubergines into 3cm thick slices and brush with groundnut oil on both sides. Preheat the grill to medium and arrange the aubergine slices on a baking sheet in a single layer. Cook, positioned away from the grill, for 2 minutes on one side then turn the slices over and grill for another couple of minutes until golden and cooked through.

Smear a little topping over each of the aubergine slices and pop them under the grill for a further 2 minutes or so. You want the topping to be caramelised and bubbling.

Scatter the grilled aubergines with shredded spring onions, cress and sesame seeds and serve with some steamed rice and pickled ginger.

If you've fallen into the habit of boiling or steaming cauliflower, try this idea. It takes mere minutes of pan-frying, and the humble brassica's best nutty, sweet notes are magically unlocked. It may seem simple, but its depth of flavour justifies its place as a stand-alone meal.

Charred baby cauliflower with cumin, chilli and almonds

SERVES 4
PREPARATION TIME: 10 MINUTES
COOKING TIME: 10 MINUTES

3 tablespoons olive oil

4 baby cauliflowers, separated into small florets

1½ teaspoons cumin seeds

2 garlic cloves, finely sliced

1 red chilli, deseeded and finely sliced

100g flaked almonds

1 tablespoon extra virgin olive oil

2 tablespoons chopped flat leaf parsley

Using a large wok or a deep frying pan, heat the olive oil and add the cauliflower, frying until darkly golden at the edges. Reduce the heat, cover with a lid or a baking sheet and cook for 1–2 minutes.

Add the cumin seeds, garlic, chilli and almonds. Stir-fry for 5 minutes over a medium heat until the almonds are golden. Season generously with salt and pepper, drizzle with the extra virgin olive oil and scatter with parsley.

This is an easy recipe that hardly needs to meet the heat, and ideal for an Indian summer when celeriac is just coming into season. The yoghurt in the dressing makes this lighter than traditional rémoulades; if you need more sustenance, serve it with some griddled bread.

Celeriac rémoulade with capers and grain mustard

SERVES 4
PREPARATION TIME: 20 MINUTES

1 medium celeriac, about 600g

juice of 1 lemon

1 egg yolk

1 teaspoon wholegrain mustard

100ml mild olive oil

2 heaped tablespoons plain yoghurt

2 teaspoons finely chopped
flat leaf parsley, plus extra, to serve

2 teaspoons finely chopped chives

2 tablespoons baby capers,
plus a few extra, to serve

a few red chicory or radicchio
leaves, to serve

Cut the celeriac into quarters and use a vegetable peeler to pare it into wide ribbons. Stack a few ribbons on top of each other to form small piles and slice into fine matchsticks. Fill a mixing bowl with water and lemon juice, and add the shredded celeriac as you go to prevent it from turning brown.

Use a mini food processor or a bowl and a whisk to make the dressing: start by blending the egg yolk with a large pinch of sea salt, the mustard and 2 tablespoons of the lemon juice. Slowly begin adding the olive oil, drop by drop at first, as you blend or whisk, slowly graduating to a thin, steady stream. When the mixture is thick and all the oil has been added, stir in the yoghurt and chopped herbs. Add the rinsed, drained and roughly chopped capers, along with some freshly ground black pepper. Taste and season with extra lemon juice or perhaps a little salt if needed.

Blanch the celeriac in plenty of boiling water for 30 seconds then tip into a colander and refresh under cold running water. Drain thoroughly and pat dry with a clean tea towel. Toss with the dressing in a large mixing bowl, divide between serving plates with the red chicory leaves and scatter with extra parsley and capers.

Perfectly cooked tofu will absorb very little oil so that it emerges from the pan golden, crisp and light. The trick is to press the tofu and dry it very thoroughly before cooking it briefly. Keep your oil hot and place the cooked tofu on absorbent kitchen paper when it's done.

Crispy five-spice tofu with soy dipping sauce

SERVES 4
PREPARATION TIME: 20 MINUTES
COOKING TIME: 10 MINUTES

FOR THE TOFU:

500g firm tofu

6 tablespoons cornflour

2 tablespoons five-spice powder

1 teaspoon dried chilli flakes

5 tablespoons groundnut oil

FOR THE SOY DIPPING SAUCE:

4 tablespoons soy sauce

2 tablespoons rice wine vinegar

1 teaspoon toasted sesame oil

2cm piece ginger, very finely chopped

1 teaspoon caster sugar

Place the tofu on a plate lined with a double layer of absorbent kitchen paper. Cover the tofu with another double layer of kitchen paper, followed by a plate, and press down firmly. Weigh the plate down with a couple of unopened tins and set aside while you prepare the rest of the recipe. Turn the oven on to a very low setting – you only need to keep the cooked tofu warm.

To make the soy dipping sauce, combine all the ingredients in a bowl, stirring to dissolve the sugar.

Now continue with the tofu. Combine the cornflour, five-spice and chilli flakes on a plate and spread out evenly. Measure half the oil into a large, stable wok and set over a low-medium flame to heat slowly. Pat the tofu dry with more absorbent kitchen paper and cut into large cubes. Roll the cubes in the cornflour mixture until well coated on all sides. Turn up the heat under the wok and fry half the tofu cubes, turning carefully with tongs, until crisp and golden on all sides. This will take about 5 minutes. Transfer to a plate lined with absorbent kitchen paper to soak up any excess oil and place in the oven to keep warm. Repeat with the remaining oil and tofu then serve straight away with the dipping sauce alongside.

Fast

Protein-rich tofu has a mild and delicate flavour, making it the ideal carrier for other tastes like sesame, soy, chilli, ginger and garlic. Depending on how firm your tofu is, you can slice it and add to things like salads and stir-fries.

How to make tofu

nigari + H₂O

70°C-80°C

tofu curds

step 1.

Pour 500ml unsweetened soy milk into a pan and boil for about 5 minutes. Stand a liquid thermometer in the pan and allow the milk to cool to between 70°C and 80°C (160–175°F).

step 2.

Dissolve 2 teaspoons of powdered nigari in 100ml lukewarm water and gradually add to the soy milk, stirring constantly. If you can't find nigari, use 50ml white wine vinegar or lemon juice and no water. The soy milk will begin to separate and curdle and look like curds and whey.

step 3.

Remove from the heat and leave well alone for 15 minutes. Large curds should have formed, but if they look small, stir in another teaspoon of dissolved nigari. Ladle out some of the liquid tofu whey and discard. Line a colander with 2 layers of damp muslin and stand in a large bowl to catch any liquid. Carefully ladle the solid tofu curds into the colander.

soy beans

Soy milk, made from soy beans, forms the basis of making tofu. Nigari (magnesium chloride) is a tofu coagulator that causes the soy milk to separate into curds and whey, rather like the process in cheese making. Powdered nigari can be found in Japanese food shops but you can use white wine vinegar or lemon juice instead, adding extra as needed until the soy milk curdles.

tofu

water

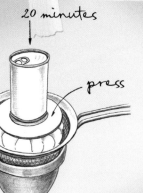

20 minutes

press

step 4.

Sit a small plate on top, weigh it down with unopened tins and leave for 20 minutes to firm up.

step 5.

Carefully unmould the drained tofu into a bowl of cold water to remove any bitterness. Soak for 10 minutes, then refresh with new water and leave to soak for a further 10 minutes.

cold water

step 6.

Use straight away or gently transfer the tofu to a lidded container, cover with cold water and chill for up to 3 days.

The little ear shapes of orecchiette collect robust sauces better than any other pasta shape, but any small shell-like variety will work well. Don't be scared of cooking the broccoli until truly soft – it doesn't take long and this is not the time for fancy, al dente vegetables.

Orecchiette pasta with broccoli and pine nuts

SERVES 4
PREPARATION TIME: 15 MINUTES
COOKING TIME: 15 MINUTES

200g purple sprouting or tenderstem broccoli, roughly chopped

350g dried orecchiette pasta

4 tablespoons extra virgin olive oil

1 chilli, deseeded and finely chopped

2 fat garlic cloves, finely sliced

75g pine nuts, toasted until golden

2 tablespoons finely grated pecorino

Blanch the broccoli in plenty of boiling water for 3 minutes or so. Drain in a colander and refresh under cold running water. Drain again and roughly chop.

Cook the orecchiette in plenty of salted boiling water for 9–11 minutes until al dente, or according to pack instructions. While the pasta cooks, combine the olive oil, chilli and garlic in a cold frying pan, place over a medium heat and cook until the garlic is fragrant but not browned. Add the chopped broccoli, cover with a lid or baking sheet, and cook very gently for a few minutes. Season well with salt and pepper and stir in the pine nuts.

Drain the pasta, reserving a couple of tablespoons of the cooking water. Tip into the frying pan with the broccoli mixture and add the pecorino and reserved cooking water. Mix well and serve.

These crisp and tender potato cakes are divine served with softly poached eggs and a punchy salsa verde. The trick to neat poached eggs is to use the freshest you can find. If you make the potato cakes a few hours ahead of time, cooking them will be a breeze.

Salad potato griddle cakes with olives and poached eggs

SERVES 4
PREPARATION TIME: 10 MINUTES
PLUS COOLING TIME
COOKING TIME: 25 MINUTES

500g small salad potatoes, such as Charlotte, Ratte or Pink Fir Apple

2 shallots, very finely chopped

2 tablespoons black olives, pitted and roughly chopped

1 tablespoon chopped flat leaf parsley

50g pecorino sardo, shaved

5 very fresh eggs

1 heaped tablespoon potato flour or plain flour, plus extra to dust

3–4 tablespoons olive oil

4 tablespoons salsa verde dressing (see page 238)

Scrub the potatoes and boil in their skins in salted water for 15 minutes, or until just tender. Drain, allow to cool for 15 minutes and then crush roughly with a fork. Add the shallots, olives, parsley and half the cheese. Season generously with freshly ground black pepper and just a little salt, and taste the mixture to make sure the seasoning is balanced. Beat 1 egg and mix into the potatoes along with the flour. Form the mixture into 8 flat cakes using floured hands.

Space the cakes out on a plate and chill for at least 1 hour or overnight. Before cooking, generously brush the potato cakes with olive oil on both sides. Heat a large griddle pan and slowly brown the cakes for about 4 minutes on each side, in batches if necessary. Keep warm while you cook the remaining eggs.

Heat a deep frying pan of water until it just reaches boiling point then reduce the heat so the base is covered in tiny bubbles. Carefully crack in the eggs, one by one, as gently as you can. Poach the eggs for 3 minutes until the whites are just set, then remove from the pan with a slotted spoon and drain on absorbent kitchen paper.

Serve a poached egg on each pair of cakes with the salsa verde spooned over with the remaining pecorino shavings.

Fast

Even though fried rice is pretty quick to make, you need to start the day before, as cooked, chilled rice is essential to get the authentic fried rice texture. Use rice left over from another dish if you have some, but ensure it's no more than one day old, and was chilled within an hour of cooking. Once the rice is done, the rest is easy.

Cashew fried rice

SERVES 4
PREPARATION TIME: 10 MINUTES
PLUS CHILLING TIME
COOKING TIME: 25 MINUTES

500g cold, cooked Thai fragrant or basmati rice (or 240g uncooked rice)

400g mixed vegetables, such as sugar snap peas, mangetout, baby sweetcorn, peas

2 tablespoons groundnut oil

100g shelled cashews

2 garlic cloves, finely chopped

4cm piece ginger, finely chopped

1–2 tablespoons soy sauce

2 eggs, beaten

1 teaspoon toasted sesame oil

chilli tomato jam (see page 242), to serve

If using the uncooked rice, start the day before. Rinse the rice well in a sieve held under cold running water and place the drained rice in a saucepan. Add enough cold water to cover the rice by about 2cm. Bring to the boil and simmer for 10 minutes until the water is absorbed. Cover the pan, remove from the heat and set aside to steam for 10 minutes. Fluff the rice up with a fork and as soon as it's cool, cover with clingfilm and chill overnight.

When you're ready to fry the rice, blanch the vegetables in boiling water for 2 minutes. Drain in a colander and refresh under cold running water.

Heat the oil in a wok, throw in the cashews and stir-fry until golden. Remove to a bowl with a slotted spoon. Add the garlic and ginger to the wok and cook for a minute, then add the cold rice and vegetables, and stir-fry for a good 2 minutes to heat through. Push everything to the side of the pan and tip in the egg and sesame oil, stirring occasionally to form a sort of omelette. Break the omelette into pieces with the spatula and mix into the rice, then add the cashews. Season with the soy sauce and serve with the chilli tomato jam on the side.

It's official: celeriac chips trump soldiers for dunking into softly boiled duck eggs, and turn breakfast fare into a stylish supper. Hands-on cooking time is minimal so while the chips get on with crisping themselves in the oven, you have a chance to relax and unwind after work.

Soft-boiled duck egg with fat celeriac dipping chips

SERVES 2
PREPARATION TIME: 15 MINUTES
COOKING TIME: 35 MINUTES

1 large celeriac, about 800g, thickly sliced

2 tablespoons mild olive oil

1 teaspoon celery salt, plus extra for the eggs

a pinch of cayenne pepper

2 duck eggs

Preheat the oven to 230°C (450°F/Gas 8). Cut the celeriac slices into fat chips and plunge into a pan of salted, boiling water for 2 minutes. Drain in a colander then coat with the olive oil, celery salt and cayenne pepper. Spread out in a single layer on a large baking sheet and bake for about 30 minutes.

When the chips are 25 minutes into their cooking time, lower the duck eggs into a saucepan of boiling water and simmer gently for 6 minutes. Remove from the water and gingerly (they'll be hot!) slice the tops off. Sit each egg in an egg cup ready for dipping. Sprinkle with a little more celery salt and accompany with golden celeriac chips fresh from the oven.

Fast

Rigatoni is a ridged, tube-shaped pasta that goes perfectly with this comforting walnut sauce. It's not chilli hot, merely warm and toasty, making it the perfect fast food for a crisp autumn night. Serve the pasta with a tangle of buttery spinach on the side if you wish.

Chilli and crushed walnut rigatoni

SERVES 4
PREPARATION TIME: 15 MINUTES
COOKING TIME: 15 MINUTES

300g walnut halves

1 tablespoon extra virgin olive oil

1 red chilli, deseeded and finely chopped

½ garlic clove, crushed

1 teaspoon thyme leaves

2 heaped tablespoons mascarpone

2 tablespoons finely grated Parmesan

350g dried rigatoni pasta or similar short pasta shapes

Toast the walnuts in a dry frying pan, tossing often until golden and fragrant. Tip onto a chopping board and when cool enough, roughly chop. Some nuts should be very fine, and some larger.

Place the olive oil, chilli and garlic in a cold frying pan and heat gently – you don't want the garlic to colour. After a minute or 2 remove the pan from the heat, stir in the thyme, followed by the mascarpone and Parmesan. Season with salt and pepper. Stir in nearly all the walnuts – keeping a couple of tablespoons back – and set aside.

Cook the pasta until al dente in a pan of salted, boiling water according to pack instructions. Drain in a colander, reserving a few tablespoons of cooking water, and immediately return the pasta to the saucepan with the reserved water. Add the walnut sauce and toss through. Serve with the reserved walnuts sprinkled over.

Tomatoes

2

Panzanella burrata

Roughly dice 3 ripe vine tomatoes and mix with 150g sourdough bread, torn into chunks and toasted in the oven. Dress with extra virgin olive oil, red wine vinegar, salt, pepper and fresh basil. Rest at room temperature for 1–2 hours. Mix in half a small, finely chopped onion and serve spooned over a globe of fresh burrata or buffalo mozzarella.

1

Simple salad

Halve or slice a plateful of tomato varieties, depending on their size, and spread out on a serving plate. Whisk 50ml single cream into 50ml olive oil with 2 tablespoons white wine vinegar, a pinch each of caster sugar and salt, and plenty of cracked black pepper. Drizzle over the tomatoes and scatter with fresh mint.

Shopska salad

Core and dice 4 large tomatoes, chop 2 deseeded red peppers, and cube 15cm of peeled and deseeded cucumber. Slice ½ small red onion very finely, and finely chop 2 tablespoons parsley leaves. Combine the tomatoes, peppers, cucumber, red onion and parsley and dress with red wine vinegar, mild olive oil, salt and pepper. Coarsely grate 100g feta over the top before serving.

3

Take Six

4

Tomato and tarragon tart

Preheat the oven to 180°C (350°F/Gas 4). Line a 12 x 35cm tart tin with shortcrust pastry, line this with paper and baking beans and bake for 15 minutes. Remove the beans and paper. Whisk 3 eggs with 190ml single cream and 1 tablespoon chopped tarragon. Season well. Stir in 3 skinned, deseeded and diced tomatoes. Spoon into the pastry case and bake for 25 minutes, or until just set.

5

Cherry tomato tart tatin

Preheat the oven to 190°C (375°F/Gas 5). Place a 15cm ovenproof frying pan over a low heat and add 2 tablespoons olive oil, 90g golden caster sugar and 250g whole cherry tomatoes. Fry until the sugar caramelises to a deep golden colour, then add 2 tablespoons balsamic vinegar. Remove from the heat and season. Tuck an 18cm circle of rolled-out puff pastry over and around the tomatoes and bake for about 15 minutes until the pastry is cooked. Carefully turn out onto a plate while still warm and serve with spoonfuls of the walnut tarator on page 241.

6

Tomato and spinach dhal

Bring 250g rinsed red lentils and 900ml water to the boil in a large pan and simmer for 10 minutes. Add 1 x 400g tin plum tomatoes, ½ teaspoon ground turmeric, 4cm grated ginger, 2 crushed garlic cloves, 1 teaspoon cumin seeds and 2 chopped green chillies. Stir, then simmer gently for 15–20 minutes, stirring often. Fold in 200g young leaf spinach, a squeeze of lime juice and salt and pepper. Eat warm with steamed rice or Indian flatbread.

One Pots
and Bakes

Chapter Seven

The grated parsnip gradually melts into the rice in this buttery but light risotto. A couple of fried sage leaves will elevate this into posh dinner territory. You could go one further with parsnip crisps: slice parsnips very thin with a vegetable peeler, coat in olive oil and roast at 160°C (315°F/Gas 2–3) for 25–30 minutes, turning halfway, until crisp.

Parsnip, sage and mascarpone risotto

SERVES 4
PREPARATION TIME: 10 MINUTES
COOKING TIME: 25 MINUTES

1 litre vegetable stock (see page 236) or quality bought stock

40g butter

2 shallots, finely chopped

2 large parsnips, coarsely grated

4 small sage leaves, finely shredded

250g risotto rice, ideally Vialone Nano

1 small glass dry white wine

2 tablespoons mascarpone, plus extra to serve

60g Parmesan, finely grated

parsnip crisps, to serve (optional)

Pour the vegetable stock into a saucepan and bring it up to simmering point. Reduce the heat to low to keep the stock hot.

In another pan, melt the butter and add the shallots, parsnips and sage. Cook gently, stirring, for 5 minutes until the shallots are soft but not coloured. Stir in the rice to coat thoroughly with the buttery vegetables and cook for a minute. Pour in the wine and stir until it evaporates, then start adding the hot stock, a ladleful at a time, stirring after each addition of stock until it virtually disappears. Continue this process for 18–20 minutes, or until the rice grains are plump but retain a bit of 'bite' and the risotto is creamy. You may not need all the stock.

Remove from the heat and swirl in half the mascarpone and grated Parmesan. Cover and set aside for 5 minutes. Mix through the remaining cheeses and serve with an extra spoonful of mascarpone on top, with a scattering of parsnip crisps (if using).

One Pots and Bakes

This is a cunning way to cook pizza at a very high temperature, and hotter than most domestic ovens will allow. By doing it this way, the already-griddled crust gets even crisper and pleasingly charred as the cheese melts – and you don't need to buy your own pizza oven.

Grilled vegetable pizza

SERVES 2–4
PREPARATION TIME: 20 MINUTES
PLUS RESTING TIME
COOKING TIME: 15 MINUTES

FOR THE PIZZA BASE:

250g strong white flour

½ teaspoon dried fast-action yeast

¾ teaspoon salt

2 tablespoons extra virgin olive oil, plus extra to oil the bowl

160–175ml lukewarm water

FOR THE TOPPING:

2 small courgettes, very finely sliced

1 fennel bulb, finely sliced

4 rosemary sprigs, leaves stripped

2 tablespoons extra virgin olive oil

2 tablespoons polenta or cornmeal

2 balls buffalo mozzarella, torn into pieces

Start by making the dough for the pizza base. Combine the dry ingredients in a large mixing bowl and add the olive oil as well as enough of the warm water to form a soft, shaggy dough. Use a wooden spoon and then your hands to blend the mixture. Turn out onto a clean, lightly floured surface and knead for 10 minutes until the dough is smooth, elastic and bouncy. Oil the bowl and return the dough to it, then cover with a clean, damp tea towel and leave in a warm place for an hour.

Meanwhile, preheat the grill to medium. Coat the vegetables and rosemary in a little olive oil and season well. Spread out in an oiled baking tray and grill for about 4 minutes, turning halfway. Set aside but keep the grill on. Ensure the shelf is at the top and close to the grill.

Place a very sturdy, large frying pan or griddle over a high heat – a thick, cast-iron pan is ideal. Leave it on the hob for at least 10 minutes as it needs to get smoking hot.

Knock the dough back to let the air out, divide it in half and gently press and stretch each piece into a rough circle, a little bit smaller than your hot pan. It should be thin – about 5mm. Lay each circle of dough on a sheet of baking paper sprinkled with a tablespoon of polenta or cornmeal. Cover the pizza bases with the grilled vegetables and the torn mozzarella then drizzle with a little olive oil.

Slide the pizzas off the paper and into the smoking hot pan. Leave for a minute, then transfer the pan to the hot grill (you'll need oven gloves!) and cook for about 4 minutes. Slide the pizza out and place the pan back on a high heat while you slice the cooked pizza into wedges. Cook the second pizza in the same way while you eat the first.

These light and fluffy little parcels don't have to be baked – you could serve them straight away with the melted herb butter or perhaps the Gorgonzola sauce on page 240. All you'll need to accompany them is a crisp salad, which will cut through the buttery richness.

Ricotta gnocchi gratin with parsley butter

SERVES 4
PREPARATION TIME: 30 MINUTES
PLUS DRAINING TIME
COOKING TIME: 13–18 MINUTES

450g ricotta

2 eggs, beaten

15g butter, melted

a few gratings of nutmeg

40g Parmesan, finely grated

about 100g plain flour, plus extra for dusting

100g parsley butter (see page 234), diced

It's very important to drain the ricotta thoroughly so try to do this the day before. Line a colander with muslin and lay the ricotta in it. Set over a bowl, cover and leave to drain for 8–24 hours. Alternatively, put the ricotta in a square of muslin and gather the material up into a ball. Squeeze firmly to force the water out. Place the cheese in a colander and weigh it down with a small plate and a couple of unopened tins to force more water out. Set aside for 20 minutes, then wring out again before you unwrap it. Turn the drained cheese into a bowl and mash with a fork. Add the eggs, butter, nutmeg and 15g of the grated Parmesan. Season with salt and pepper then fork through to mix lightly but evenly.

Measure the flour onto a plate. Drop heaped teaspoonfuls of the ricotta mixture into the flour – do them in batches of about 5 or so. Turn them over with a fork then fish the bundles out one by one and gently jiggle each of them in your hand to form lightly floured ovals. Don't squeeze or press. Place on a lightly floured tray and repeat. You can cook the gnocchi straight away or chill for an hour or so to firm them.

Put half the parsley butter in a heatproof bowl and preheat the oven to 200°C (400°F/Gas 6). Bring a large, wide saucepan of generously salted water to a simmer, drop in the gnocchi one by one, and cook until they float to the surface – this will take about 3 minutes. Remove the gnocchi from the pan with a slotted spoon, shaking excess water off, and drop them into the bowl of parsley butter. Toss gently to melt the butter, then tip into a medium gratin dish. Dot with the remaining parsley butter cubes and shower with the rest of the grated Parmesan. Bake for 10–15 minutes until golden and bubbling. Serve with a simple green salad.

Toasting before steaming or simmering adds a whole new dimension to couscous. The main thing to bear in mind is that you must season it generously. Herbs, citrus zest, spices and good olive oil will also give the toasted grain a nudge along in the flavour stakes.

Baked red onions stuffed with toasted, spiced couscous

SERVES 4
PREPARATION TIME: 20 MINUTES
COOKING TIME: 1 HOUR 40 MINUTES

4 large red onions, skins on

2 tablespoons olive oil, plus extra for drizzling

30g butter

½ teaspoon ground cinnamon

3 tablespoons uncooked couscous

300ml vegetable stock (see page 236) or quality bought stock

2 tablespoons chopped dried apricots

2 tablespoons pine nuts, toasted in a dry pan

1 tablespoon chopped flat leaf parsley

Preheat the oven to 200°C (400°F/Gas 6). Cut the tops off the onions and reserve. Slice any fibres off the root ends of the onions so they can sit upright, but leave as intact as possible so the onions hold together. Place in a baking dish or casserole, pour in a wine glass of water and drizzle with olive oil. Cover with foil or a lid and bake for 1 hour, then uncover and set aside. When just cool enough to handle, scoop out the onion centres with a teaspoon, leaving enough outside layers to form a thick shell. Roughly chop the scooped-out flesh.

Heat the 2 tablespoons of olive oil and 15g of the butter in a frying pan. Add the chopped, scooped-out onion plus the cinnamon and couscous. Stir for a few minutes until the couscous turns golden. Add 100ml stock, season generously with salt and pepper, and remove from the heat. Set aside for 5 minutes then add the apricots, pine nuts and parsley and mix well.

Spoon this mixture into the hollowed-out onions in the cooking dish, and pop the onion tops in the dish as well, along with the remaining stock. Dot with the remaining 15g butter and bake uncovered for 25 minutes until golden. Cover the onions with foil or a lid if the tops brown too much before the cooking time is up. Perch the tops back on the onions to serve if you like.

Chestnuts aren't just for Christmas, although this would make a very good Yuletide side dish. Waxy potatoes or chunks of celeriac or parsnip can replace the Jerusalem artichokes if you prefer.

Braised, buttered chestnuts with Jerusalem artichokes

SERVES 3–4
PREPARATION TIME: 15 MINUTES
COOKING TIME: 30 MINUTES

500g Jerusalem artichokes

a squeeze of lemon

60g butter

1 sweet white onion, finely sliced

2 garlic cloves, unpeeled and bruised

4 bay leaves

200g cooked and peeled chestnuts
(vacuum-packed are fine)

1 small glass red wine

1 small glass vegetable stock
(see page 236) or quality bought stock

Start by peeling the Jerusalem artichokes. Cut them into 2cm slices and submerge in a bowlful of cold water spiked with a squeeze of lemon.

Melt the butter in a large casserole or deep-sided frying pan and add the onion. Cook gently for 5 minutes until softened. Add the garlic cloves, bay leaves and thoroughly drained artichokes, followed by the chestnuts and a little salt and pepper. Stir to coat the vegetables in the butter. Cover the pan and cook for 10 minutes, stirring occasionally. Then add the wine and stock, and bring to the boil. Simmer for 10 minutes, or until the artichokes are tender and the liquid reduced. Check the seasoning.

You can use a fork to crush the sweet and mild cooked garlic cloves into the sauce before serving to add body and depth. There won't be any hint of harsh garlic flavour – just fish out and discard the papery skin.

Serve with steamed greens and perhaps some puréed potatoes if you are particularly hungry.

Undercooked aubergines are disappointing indeed, but there's little chance of that happening here. Fried until crisp and golden then braised, these are silky smooth and tender – just as they should be.

Braised baby aubergines with bok choy, peanuts and Thai basil

SERVES 4
PREPARATION TIME: 15 MINUTES
COOKING TIME: 10–15 MINUTES

100ml groundnut oil

12 baby aubergines, halved

2 garlic cloves, chopped

3cm piece ginger, finely chopped

6 heads baby bok choy, halved

4 spring onions, sliced

2 tablespoons light soy sauce

2 teaspoons palm sugar or light brown sugar

3 tablespoons peanuts, toasted and crushed

a small handful of Thai basil leaves

Score the flesh of the aubergines in a crisscross pattern, then heat the oil in a large wok until it shimmers. Add the aubergines and fry, turning with tongs, until deeply golden. Remove to a plate lined with absorbent kitchen paper then carefully pour most of the oil out of the wok, leaving about a tablespoonful behind.

Return the wok to the heat and add the garlic and ginger. Stir-fry for half a minute then add the bok choy and spring onions. Continue to stir-fry for a minute or so more.

Return the aubergines to the wok with the soy sauce, plus the palm or brown sugar and 2 tablespoons water. Allow to bubble and thicken for a couple more minutes.

Scatter with crushed peanuts and Thai basil and serve with steamed rice.

This Malaysian egg curry is fragrant and feisty, requiring only steamed rice to serve. Traditionally, the eggs would be hard-boiled but this dish is far more delicious when they're a little soft inside. To soft boil eggs, cover them with cold water in a saucepan and place over a medium heat. As soon as the water boils, remove from the heat and set aside for seven minutes. Refresh in cool water and peel carefully.

Sambal Telur

SERVES 4
PREPARATION TIME: 15 MINUTES
COOKING TIME: 15 MINUTES

3 vine-ripened tomatoes

1 tablespoon groundnut oil

4 shallots, finely sliced

3 garlic cloves, chopped

4cm piece ginger, finely chopped

1 teaspoon coriander seeds, crushed

1 teaspoon cumin seeds, crushed

½ teaspoon ground turmeric

1 tablespoon sambal oelek

1 x 400ml tin coconut milk

2 tablespoons tamarind pulp

1 tablespoon palm sugar or brown sugar

8 eggs, soft-boiled

2 tablespoons fried shallots, to serve

Cut a shallow cross in the base of the tomatoes with a sharp knife and place them in a bowl. Cover with boiling water and leave for a minute. Drain and peel, then roughly chop the flesh and set aside.

Heat the oil in a wok or saucepan, add the shallots, garlic and ginger and cook for a minute. Add the coriander, cumin, turmeric, sambal oelek and the chopped tomatoes and sauté for a few minutes more.

Stir in the coconut milk, tamarind pulp and palm sugar along with a hefty pinch of salt. Bring to the boil and simmer for 5 minutes until the mixture thickens.

Add the eggs and simmer for a few more minutes to heat them through. Scatter with fried shallots and serve the curry with steamed rice.

Side dishes

2

Green papaya salad

Peel a large green papaya and shred the flesh. Add to a bowl with 1 large shredded carrot and dress with a few tablespoons of ginger and lime dipping sauce (see page 244). Toss through a couple of spoonfuls of Thai basil leaves, and top with chopped, toasted peanuts or cashews.

1

Greens dressed with walnut tarator

Plunge some seasonal greens – any type of kale or cabbage, broccoli, chard or bok choy – into salted water and simmer until just tender. Drain and dress the vegetables with walnut tarator (see page 241).

Asparagus with brioche crumbs

Cook trimmed green asparagus spears in salted water until just tender. Melt a generous knob of butter in a frying pan and add finely whizzed brioche crumbs with the grated zest of ½ lemon. Stir and toast until golden. Season and scatter over the drained asparagus. You could also serve the cooked asparagus with blender hollandaise or Gorgonzola sauce (see page 240).

3

4

Red cabbage slaw with gomashio

Slice ½ medium red cabbage very finely and finely slice a quartered, cored red apple. Dress with a little toasted sesame oil, rice vinegar and soy sauce. Toss through a few coriander leaves and scatter with gomashio (see page 236). This also goes splendidly with grilled sweetcorn or shredded carrot.

5

Beetroot and fig carpaccio with tapenade dressing

Slice 4 raw peeled beetroot into paper-thin slices and slice 3 ripe figs as thinly as you can without the flesh breaking. Place on a plate and scatter with a few lemon thyme leaves. Combine 2 tablespoons fig tapenade (see page 240) with 1 tablespoon red wine vinegar, 1 tablespoon extra virgin olive oil and 1 tablespoon water. Spoon over the beetroot and figs and season lightly to finish.

6

Spiced sweet potato wedges

Preheat the oven to 200°C (400°F/Gas 6). Peel 600g sweet potatoes, or leave the skin on if you wish, and slice into wedges. Toss the wedges in 3 tablespoons olive oil, 2 crushed garlic cloves, 1 tablespoon each crushed cumin, fennel and coriander seeds and a pinch of dried chilli flakes. Season and spread out on a baking tray. Bake for 35 minutes or so, turning halfway. Serve the potatoes as they are or with parsley or rocket pesto (see page 238).

Sometimes only a comforting, familiar supper will do. Make the whole thing in advance to reheat when needed if you wish, or just pre-prepare the crêpes. Stack them, each one separated by baking paper, and keep well-wrapped in the refrigerator for a day or two.

Spinach, herb and ricotta crêpes gratin

SERVES 4
PREPARATION TIME: 20 MINUTES
PLUS STANDING TIME
COOKING TIME: ABOUT 30 MINUTES

FOR THE CRÊPES:

275ml milk

2 eggs, beaten

30g butter, melted, plus a little extra to cook the crêpes

60g plain wholemeal flour

60g buckwheat flour

FOR THE FILLING:

30g butter, plus extra for greasing

200g spinach leaves, washed and dried

250g ricotta, drained

2 tablespoons roughly chopped soft herbs, such as chives, basil or parsley

a good grating of nutmeg

4 tablespoons finely grated Parmesan

1 quantity rustic, slow-roast tomato sauce (see page 242)

1 ball buffalo mozzarella, torn into pieces

Start with the crêpes. Whisk the milk, eggs and butter into the flours with a pinch of salt to make a smooth batter, or whizz the ingredients together in a blender. Transfer to a jug and if you have time, leave the batter to stand for 20 minutes or so. Place a medium frying pan over the heat and add a small knob of butter. When it melts and sizzles, pour a small ladleful (about 2 tablespoons) of stirred batter into the pan and swirl to cover the base completely so you form a thin crêpe. Allow to cook for a minute or so then flip and cook for a minute more. Slide onto a plate and repeat to make 8 pancakes. Stack the cooked crêpes on top of each other, separated by squares of baking paper to stop them sticking.

Grease a large gratin dish and preheat the oven to 200°C (400°F/Gas 6).

To make the filling, wilt the spinach in the butter and remove from the heat. Once cooled a little, roughly chop the spinach and stir into the ricotta with the herbs, nutmeg and half the Parmesan. Spoon an eighth of the mixture onto the centre of each crêpe and fold in half then in half again to form a fan shape. Place the filled crêpes in the buttered gratin dish and spoon the tomato sauce over. Scatter with the remaining Parmesan and the torn mozzarella and bake for 20 minutes or so until the cheese is golden and bubbling.

This is nourishing comfort food at its finest. It's a meltingly delicious dish, which has an appealingly sweet combination of flavours that children love, but the addition of some waxy potato would temper it a little. Of course, feel free to vary the root vegetables as you wish.

Shredded root vegetable gratin with crème fraîche and Gruyère

SERVES 4–6
PREPARATION TIME: 20 MINUTES
COOKING TIME: 40 MINUTES

1 garlic clove, halved

soft butter, for greasing

500g butternut squash or pumpkin, deseeded and shredded

200g carrots, shredded

200g parsnips, shredded

200g sweet potato, shredded

400ml crème fraîche

100ml dry white wine

120g Gruyère, coarsely grated

2 teaspoons thyme leaves

Preheat the oven to 200°C (400°F/Gas 6). Rub the cut garlic around the inside of a deep, medium-sized gratin dish. Discard the garlic clove and smear the dish with butter.

Place half the shredded vegetables in the dish, pressing them down firmly to expel as much air as possible. You can keep the vegetable layers distinct, or mix all the varieties together as you wish. Either way, season the layers well with salt and pepper.

Mix the crème fraîche and wine together and season with salt and pepper. Spoon half this mixture over the vegetables and top with a third of the grated Gruyère. Scatter half the thyme over, and top with the remaining vegetables, pressing down firmly as before. Pour the remaining crème fraîche mixture over, scatter with a little salt, pepper and the remaining thyme, and finish with the last 80g Gruyère.

Cover with foil, seal well and bake for 30 minutes. Uncover, then bake for a further 30 minutes or so until golden and bubbling. Let the gratin rest and settle for at least 10 minutes before serving with a salad or steamed green vegetables.

This is a stunning, rustic starter. Should the idea of preparing fresh artichokes instil fear in your heart, don't worry, you can use the deli-style artichoke halves in oil. If you do, simply sauté the shallots and garlic, and stir in the other stuffing ingredients before spooning into the artichokes and baking for 15–20 minutes to brown. You won't need the stock.

Artichokes with lemon and oregano breadcrumbs and citrus mayonnaise

SERVES 4
PREPARATION TIME: 30 MINUTES
COOKING TIME: ABOUT 50 MINUTES

FOR THE ARTICHOKES:

12 young violet artichokes

finely grated zest and juice of 1 lemon

2 shallots, finely chopped

4 tablespoons olive oil

1 garlic clove, crushed

100g coarse sourdough breadcrumbs

1 tablespoon oregano leaves, chopped

1 glass white wine

1 glass vegetable stock (see page 236) or quality bought stock

FOR THE MAYONNAISE:

½ quantity mayonnaise (see page 236) or ½ cup quality bought mayonnaise

finely grated zest of 1 lemon

1 tablespoon lemon juice

Preheat the oven to 180°C (350°F/Gas 4). Slice the stalks from the artichokes so they will stand upright. Remove the tough outer leaves from each artichoke bud until you reach the lighter-coloured leaves beneath. Cut the spiny tops off the leaves, open the leaves out slightly and use a teaspoon to scoop out the hairy central core or choke, and discard. Drop the prepared artichokes into a bowl of cold water with the lemon juice added.

In a casserole or sturdy roasting tin, soften the shallots in 3 tablespoons olive oil until translucent. Add the garlic and cook for another minute. Scoop the mixture into a bowl and add the breadcrumbs, lemon zest and oregano along with some salt and pepper. Mix well. Remove the artichokes from the water and shake them dry. Spoon the stuffing mixture into the cavities between the leaves.

Add the remaining oil to the same casserole or tin and sit the artichokes in it. Pour in the wine and stock and cover tightly with a lid or a double layer of foil. Bake for 30 minutes then uncover and cook for a further 10–15 minutes until the breadcrumbs are golden.

Stir the lemon zest and juice into the mayonnaise and serve alongside the artichokes.

A French variation on Italian pizza, this sharply savoury tart is traditionally crisscrossed with salty anchovies. Clearly, this would not be the vegetarian way to go, so anchovies have been replaced by scarlet strips of sun-dried tomato – with anything but ill-effect.

Pissaladière

SERVES 4–6
PREPARATION TIME: 35 MINUTES
PLUS CHILLING TIME
COOKING TIME: ABOUT 1 HOUR

FOR THE FILLING:

900g onions, finely sliced

3 tablespoons olive oil

3 x 400g tins plum tomatoes, drained and roughly chopped

18 sun-dried tomatoes in oil, drained and sliced into strips

12 black olives, stoned

FOR THE PASTRY:

175g plain flour

½ teaspoon salt

90g butter, cubed

1 egg yolk

2–3 tablespoons iced water

a little flour, for dusting

Soften the onions in the olive oil in a large saucepan. Keep the heat low and the lid on the pan; the onions must not over-brown or burn at this stage, so check them often and stir regularly. When they are a pale golden colour – about 30 minutes later – remove the lid and add the chopped plum tomatoes. Turn the heat up a little and continue to cook until any liquid has evaporated and the tomatoes have started to break down.

Next, make the pastry. Place the flour, salt and butter in a food processor and pulse until the mixture is finely blended – but don't overwork it. Add the egg yolk and 2 tablespoons iced water and pulse again, adding more water by the teaspoonful until the pastry comes together to form a ball.

Preheat the oven to 190°C (375°F/Gas 5). Roll out the pastry on a lightly floured surface and transfer to a 35 x 12cm rectangular or 20cm round tart tin. Press the pastry in firmly to fit, but make sure not to stretch it or it will shrink while baking. Leave the sides untrimmed, prick the base lightly with a fork and chill for 30 minutes.

When chilled, cover the pastry case with non-stick baking paper and fill with baking beans or dried pulses. Bake for 10 minutes then remove the paper and beans and cook for another 5 minutes or so until the pastry turns a very pale gold. Remove the pastry case from the oven and once it has cooled a little, trim the edges flush with the tin using a very sharp knife.

Fill the pastry case with the onion mixture, pressing it out evenly. Use the strips of sun-dried tomato to make a crisscross pattern on top and stud the gaps with black olives. Bake for 20–25 minutes. Cover the tart with a loose sheet of foil if the pastry seems to be browning too quickly.

The ingredients are rich, but this is a delicate dish that's elegant rather than clumsy, thanks to fine layering. As with all simple food, it demands quality ingredients. Ideally, make lasagne sheets from the pasta recipe on page 216, multiplying the quantities by 1.5. Or use sheets of quality bought fresh pasta, and roll them out ethereally thin.

Fine white lasagne with many layers

SERVES 6–8
PREPARATION TIME: 40 MINUTES
PLUS INFUSING TIME
COOKING TIME: 50 MINUTES

1 quantity Béchamel sauce (see page 241)

butter for greasing

450g fresh lasagne sheets

olive oil, for dizzling

300g mushrooms, any sort, finely chopped

30g butter

1 garlic clove, crushed

a large handful of basil leaves

4 tablespoons finely grated Parmesan

2 balls buffalo mozzarella, torn into pieces

Start by making the Béchamel sauce, then cover to prevent a skin forming and set aside.

Preheat the oven to 180°C (350°F/Gas 4) and grease a medium-large ceramic lasagne dish. Cut the lasagne sheets into halves or thirds so they can be layered in the dish easily. Drop each sheet, one by one, into a saucepan of boiling, salted water. Simmer for a mere minute or 2 then drain and refresh under cold running water. Drizzle with olive oil and lay the sheets out on clean tea towels in a single layer.

Sauté the mushrooms gently in the butter for a few minutes until softened but not coloured. Stir in the garlic and cook for a further 2 minutes until much of the liquid has cooked off. Spread a little of the mixture over the base of the dish and scatter with basil leaves. Don't use much; this is all about fine and delicate layering, not thick bands of filling. Cover the mushrooms with a layer of pasta, a very thin layer of Béchamel, a little seasoning and a meagre sprinkle of Parmesan. Top with another layer of pasta then begin the layering process again, starting with the mushrooms. Continue layering like this until you have used all the ingredients, finishing with lasagne sheets, Béchamel sauce and a final layer of torn mozzarella, all dusted with some grated Parmesan.

Bake for 35 minutes or so until the lasagne is bubbling and golden at the edges.

This frittata makes a perfect supper: it's easy to prepare and allows you to put your feet up while it bakes to firmness in the oven. The barley, an unusual inclusion in frittata, is cooked until tender but still chewy. If you prefer it softer, simmer it for an extra 10 minutes.

Oven-baked pea, barley and broad bean frittata

SERVES 6
PREPARATION TIME: 15 MINUTES
COOKING TIME: 50 MINUTES

150g pearl barley

2 mint sprigs

100g shelled peas

100g broad beans, podded weight, skins removed

6 eggs, lightly beaten

3 tablespoons double cream

1 garlic clove, crushed

3 tablespoons olive oil

150g halloumi, cubed

Cover the barley with plenty of cold water. Add a pinch of salt and a sprig of mint, and bring to the boil. Simmer for 20 minutes until the barley is tender. Add the peas and broad beans and simmer for a few minutes more, then drain.

Preheat the oven to 200°C (400°F/Gas 6). Chop the remaining mint leaves and add to the eggs with the cream and crushed garlic. Season with plenty of pepper but only a little salt because the cheese is salty. Place a large, ovenproof frying pan over a medium heat and add the olive oil. Spoon the barley mixture into the pan and spread it out. Pour in the egg mixture, shaking the frying pan to distribute it evenly, and then scatter with the halloumi, pushing some of it down into the egg. Cook for a couple of minutes then pop the pan in the oven for 15–20 minutes to set the egg and brown the cheese. Rest the frittata for 5 minutes before slicing and serving.

Risottos

2

Courgette and Taleggio

Make the basic risotto bianco, but stir in a few thyme leaves and 2 trimmed and finely diced courgettes about 15 minutes into the rice cooking time. When the grains are just cooked, fold in 100g diced Taleggio with the butter and Parmesan, and set aside to rest. The cheese cubes will become molten and voluptuous as they warm through.

1

Bianco

Heat 1 litre vegetable stock. Soften 3 finely chopped shallots in 1 tablespoon olive oil and 15g butter. Add 400g risotto rice and stir to coat the rice in buttery oil. Add 2 glasses dry white wine. Stir until evaporated then add a pinch of salt and a ladleful of stock. Stir. As the stock evaporates, add more and stir, continuing for about 18 minutes until the rice is just tender. Remove from heat and stir in 50g cubed butter and 100g finely grated Parmesan. Cover and set aside for 2 minutes before serving.

Tomato and pesto

Make the basic risotto bianco but stir in 12 roughly chopped slow-roast tomato halves (see page 242) halfway through cooking the rice. Omit the butter at the end and stir in only 50g grated Parmesan. Serve each bowlful topped with a spoonful of classic pesto (see page 238), an extra roast tomato half and scatter with extra basil leaves.

3

4
Fennel and lemon

Make the basic risotto bianco but include a large, finely chopped fennel bulb and a finely chopped garlic clove with the shallots. Five minutes before the end of cooking, stir in the finely grated zest of a lemon. When the risotto is cooked, add the juice of a small lemon and replace the 50g butter with 50g mascarpone. Finish with chopped fennel tops and a grating of lemon zest.

6
Cauliflower pangrattato

Make the basic risotto bianco but add 400g cauliflower florets and a bay leaf to the stock. Simmer for 10 minutes. Add 2 crushed garlic cloves to the shallots and when adding stock to the rice, include the cauliflower. Whizz 150g sourdough bread with a pinch of dried chilli flakes, a garlic clove and 1 teaspoon thyme leaves until crumbs form. Fry with 25g butter and 2 tablespoons olive oil until golden. Serve the risotto scattered with the toasted crumbs.

5
Wild garlic

Make the basic risotto bianco and just a couple of minutes before the rice is cooked, stir in about 150g wild garlic leaves. Add the butter and cheese and continue the risotto bianco recipe as written. Serve with extra Parmesan.

Special

Chapter Eight

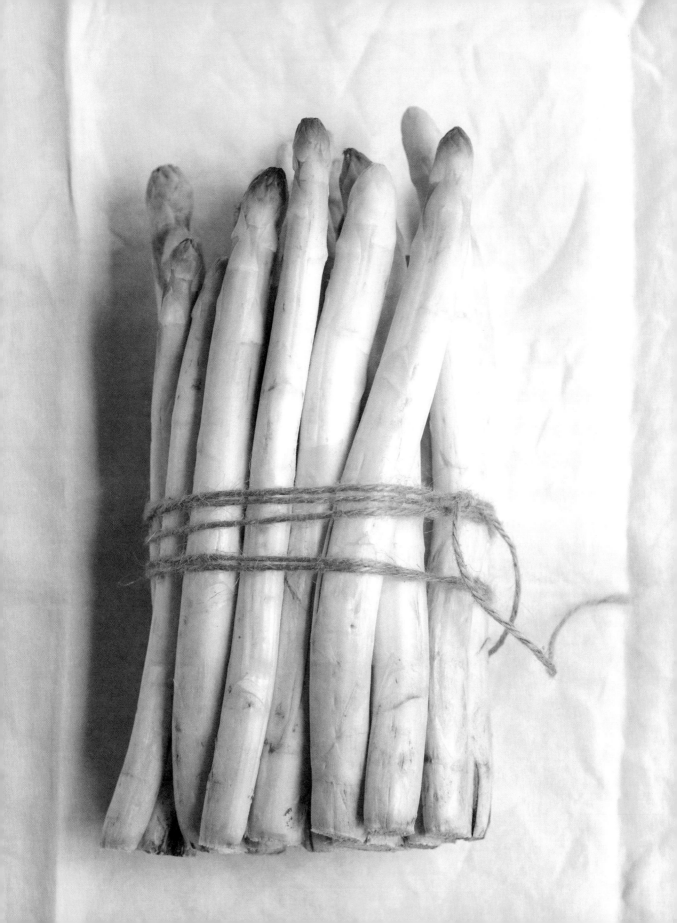

Aubergine caviar is also known as 'poor man's caviar', but that's a misnomer. True, you won't find a single fish egg here, but this is still a luxurious mouthful to serve as a canapé, or before a special dinner. And with their pomegranate jewels, they're as pretty as a picture.

Chervil pancakes with aubergine caviar and pomegranate

MAKES ABOUT 24
PREPARATION TIME: 15 MINUTES
PLUS COOLING TIME
COOKING TIME: 1 HOUR

FOR THE AUBERGINE CAVIAR:

1 garlic clove

1 teaspoon cumin seeds

2 medium aubergines, halved lengthways

3 tablespoons extra virgin olive oil

2 teaspoons pomegranate molasses or a squeeze of lemon

4 tablespoons thick Greek yoghurt

3 tablespoons fresh pomegranate seeds

FOR THE PANCAKES:

225g self-raising flour

1 teaspoon baking powder

2 eggs, beaten

260ml buttermilk

1 tablespoon chopped chervil, plus extra leaves to serve

butter, for greasing

Preheat the oven to 200°C (400°F/Gas 6). Use a pestle and mortar to crush the garlic with the cumin seeds and a large pinch of salt. Spread this mixture over the cut surfaces of the aubergines then sandwich the halves together and wrap in foil. Bake for 40 minutes until tender then unwrap and set aside to cool.

With a spoon, scoop the flesh from the aubergines into a saucepan and discard the skins. Add the olive oil and heat the pan, stirring the mixture as it simmers. Cook for 5 minutes or so to evaporate the excess water and concentrate the flavours. Leave to cool, then beat in the pomegranate molasses or lemon juice, a tablespoon of yoghurt and a little salt and pepper to taste.

Combine 2 tablespoons of the pomegranate seeds with the remaining yoghurt and set aside.

To make the pancakes, whisk all the ingredients together, except the extra chervil leaves, until smooth. Cook heaped teaspoonfuls of the mixture in a hot frying pan greased with the butter. They will take a minute or 2 on each side to cook. Flip them when the little bubbles that rise to the surface start to burst.

Place a teaspoonful of the aubergine mixture on each pancake and top with a little yoghurt. Add a few pomegranate seeds and a sprig of chervil to finish.

Special

Stéphane Reynaud has been chef proprietor of Villa9trois in Montreuil, near Paris, since 2003. His recipes combine his enthusiasm for modern cuisine with his passion for the freshest, best quality, seasonal produce. He favours these wonderful spring rolls for their simplicity, and because they can be adapted with the seasons. In winter, try using Stilton, pears, beetroot, corn salad … and so on.

Stéphane Reynaud's
Summer
spring rolls

SERVES 6
PREPARATION TIME: 30 MINUTES

FOR THE TOMATO COULIS:

4 large, very ripe tomatoes

a little olive oil

30g piece ginger, grated

1 small onion, finely chopped

4 garlic cloves, finely chopped

1 spring onion, finely chopped

FOR THE ROLLS:

200g fresh, soft goat's cheese

2 tablespoons olive oil

6 large or 12 small rice paper rounds

1 mango, peeled, stoned and sliced into matchsticks

100g soy sprouts

50g afalfa sprouts

½ cucumber, peeled, deseeded and sliced into matchsticks

a handful of rocket leaves

2 tablespoons soy sauce

Start with the tomato coulis. Cut a cross in the base of the tomatoes and cover with boiling water in a bowl and leave for 30 seconds. Drain, remove the skins and roughly chop. Pour a little olive oil into a saucepan and soften the ginger, onion and garlic over a medium heat until golden. Add the peeled tomatoes and cook gently for 20 minutes. Purée in a blender until smooth and season to taste. Set aside until ready to serve or keep in the refrigerator for up to 3 days.

To make the rolls, mix the chopped spring onion with the goat's cheese and olive oil. Spoon into a piping bag fitted with a large, straight nozzle. Place a clean, damp tea towel flat on your work surface. Soak one rice paper round at a time in lukewarm water to soften, place it on the linen and pipe a line of cheese paste along the horizontal 'edge' nearest you. Pile one-twelfth or one-sixth (depending on whether your rice paper rounds are small or large, respectively) of the mango and vegetables along this line. Fold in the vertical sides by 1cm and roll tightly away from you. Repeat until all the rice paper rounds are full.

To serve, halve the rolls (if small) or cut into 4 pieces (if large), and drop a little soy sauce onto each. Serve with the tomato coulis.

Miang Kham are traditional Thai snacks and here these delicious parcels have been repackaged slightly to become fresh and elegant canapés or starters. Betel leaves are widely used in cooking and for medicinal purposes throughout Southeast Asia.

Betel leaf wraps with coconut and cashews

MAKES 20
PREPARATION TIME: 20 MINUTES
COOKING TIME: ABOUT 10 MINUTES

50g fresh or dried shredded coconut, toasted

4cm piece ginger, finely chopped

2 Thai chillies, finely chopped

3 tablespoons chopped cashews, toasted

175g palm sugar or light brown soft sugar

60ml vegetarian fish sauce or soy sauce

2 tablespoons sieved tamarind pulp or tamarind purée

½ small lime, finely diced, including skin

1 small pomelo, flesh separated and pulled into small chunks

1 shallot, finely chopped

20 betel leaves or spinach leaves

a handful of coriander sprouts or leaves

Using a pestle and mortar or a mini food processor, grind to a paste half the coconut, half the ginger, the chillies and 2 tablespoons cashews with a pinch of salt. Set aside.

Combine the palm or brown sugar with 60ml water in a saucepan and heat gently until dissolved. Increase the heat and simmer for a few minutes until reduced to syrup. Stir in the pounded paste with the vegetarian fish sauce or soy sauce. Simmer for 3 minutes more and stir in the tamarind and heat through, then remove from the heat. Cool a little.

Mix together the lime, pomelo and shallot. Place teaspoonfuls of this mixture onto the centre of the betel leaves, shiny sides down, and add a little of the cooled tamarind mixture followed by a couple of coriander sprouts or leaves. Pinch each leaf together slightly at the base. You can use a small cocktail stick to secure them if you like.

Special

Skye Gyngell is head chef at Petersham Nurseries Cafe, in Richmond, southwest of London, a restaurant famed for its beautiful surroundings and inventive seasonal food. To make the vibrant basil oil in this recipe, whizz together leaves from 3 large bunches of basil, 1 peeled garlic clove and a good pinch each of salt and pepper. With the motor running, trickle in 200ml of extra virgin olive oil.

Skye Gyngell's
Nectarine and tomato salad with buffalo mozzarella

SERVES 4
PREPARATION TIME: 15 MINUTES

4 perfectly ripe nectarines

12 perfectly ripe heirloom tomatoes

a few drops of lemon juice

2 tablespoons good-quality extra virgin olive oil

sea salt and freshly ground black pepper

4 balls of buffalo mozzarella

12 purple basil leaves, torn or shredded

2 tablespoons basil oil
(see introduction above)

aged balsamic vinegar, to drizzle (optional)

Cut the nectarines in half along their natural division, remove the stones and cut each half into 3 wedges. Halve the tomatoes. Place the nectarines and tomatoes in a bowl and sprinkle with a few drops of lemon juice. Drizzle over the extra virgin olive oil and season with a little salt and pepper.

Tear the mozzarella balls in half with your fingers and lay 2 halves on each plate. Now build your salad, alternating the peach slices and tomatoes with basil, spooning a little basil oil between the layers and seasoning delicately as you go. Finish with a restrained drizzle of balsamic vinegar, if you like. Serve at once, preferably with really good chewy peasant-style bread drizzled with more olive oil.

White asparagus is grown in darkness below the soil surface to keep it blanched of colour, and the resulting spears are delicately flavoured. Some people add sugar to the cooking water to prevent bitterness, but simmering them in diluted milk has the same effect and won't taint the vegetable with unnecessary sweetness.

White asparagus with Champagne beurre blanc

SERVES 4
PREPARATION TIME: 10 MINUTES
COOKING TIME: 20 MINUTES

FOR THE BEURRE BLANC:

1 shallot, finely chopped

4 black peppercorns

1 tarragon sprig

175ml Champagne or dry white wine

175g butter, chilled and cubed

FOR THE ASPARAGUS:

20 white asparagus spears, about 600g

200ml milk

15g butter

Start by making the beurre blanc reduction. Place the shallot, peppercorns, tarragon and Champagne or dry white wine in a saucepan and bring to the boil. Simmer the liquid down slowly for a few minutes until reduced by two-thirds. Strain through a sieve into a heatproof bowl.

Trim the tough 2cm or so from the base of each asparagus spear. Carefully pare away the skin from the stalks (but not the tips) using a vegetable peeler, treating them gently so the spears don't snap.

Using a frying pan large enough to hold the stalks in a single layer, lay the asparagus out flat. Add the milk and 15g butter with 200ml water or enough to cover the spears. Bring to the boil and simmer for 10–12 minutes, turning the spears over occasionally until they are tender. The cooking time will depend on how thick the stalks are. Set aside in the pan.

Meanwhile, finish the beurre blanc. Set the Champagne reduction in its heatproof bowl over a pan of barely simmering water, being careful not to let the bowl come into contact with the water. Whisk in all the cubes of butter, one by one, until emulsified into a smooth sauce. Season to taste with a little salt and pepper. Remove from the heat but leave the bowl over the hot water to keep warm if you can't serve the dish straight away, stirring every now and then. The sauce will last for 10 minutes or so like this but any longer and it might split. Serve the warm sauce spooned over the drained, warm asparagus spears.

Special

Rowley Leigh, chef proprietor of Le Café Anglais in London, is one of the founding fathers of modern British cooking and a successful food writer. His elegant menus make use of French influences and techniques, but remain uncomplicated. Needless to say, this tian is only worth making with good ripe tomatoes, such as the French Marmande, Italian vine, or plum tomatoes from either country.

Rowley Leigh's
Tian of tomatoes and aubergines

SERVES 6–8
PREPARATION TIME: 30 MINUTES
COOKING TIME: 35 MINUTES

300g all-butter puff pastry

750g aubergines, sliced 5mm thick

180ml olive oil

750g ripe tomatoes

4 garlic cloves

1 small bunch flat leaf parsley, leaves finely chopped

3 tablespoons fresh breadcrumbs

Roll out the puff pastry into a disc about 23cm in diameter and leave to rest on a baking tray.

Brush the aubergine slices well with half the olive oil and cook in a dry frying pan, brushing them with a little more oil if they become dry. They should be golden and cooked through.

Peel the tomatoes by removing the cores and plunging them in boiling water for 10 seconds before refreshing them in plenty of cold water. Peel then slice the tomatoes to the same thickness as the aubergines.

Preheat the oven to 190°C (375°F/Gas 5).

Chop the garlic very finely, crushing it with the help of a teaspoon of sea salt. Mix together the garlic, parsley and breadcrumbs to make a persillade.

Arrange the tomatoes and aubergines in overlapping layers on top of the puff pastry leaving a 1.5cm border of pastry still showing. Season with a little salt and plenty of ground black pepper before sprinkling the persillade over the top. Spoon the remaining oil over the crumbs and then bake in the oven for about 35 minutes until the pastry is risen and golden. Slide onto a large serving plate and leave to cool.

  Special

Making a rotolo undoubtedly involves a bit of love and hard work, but it will repay you handsomely in flavour and compliments. If it makes life easier you can roast the pumpkin, wilt the spinach and make the pasta the day before. That way, you'll only have to assemble and simmer the rotolo and make the sage butter on the day.

Pumpkin and spinach rotolo with sage butter

SERVES 6 AS A STARTER
PREPARATION TIME: 45 MINUTES
PLUS CHILLING TIME
COOKING TIME: 1 HOUR

FOR THE PASTA:

300g type 00 flour, plus extra
for rolling out

2 eggs

2 egg yolks

FOR THE FILLING:

a handful of small sage leaves

450g peeled pumpkin, cut into
2cm cubes

3 tablespoons olive oil

600g spinach leaves, washed

75g butter

250g ricotta, drained

2 tablespoons finely grated Parmesan

a good grating of nutmeg

½ quantity slow-roast
tomatoes (see page 242), made with
500g cherry tomatoes

Pulse the pasta ingredients in a food processor until 'breadcrumbs' form, and tip onto a work surface. Knead for 5 minutes until smooth, soft and elastic. Form into a disc, wrap in clingfilm and leave in a cool place for at least 30 minutes.

Preheat the oven to 200°C (400°F/Gas 6). Shred a couple of sage leaves finely and toss with the pumpkin and 1 tablespoon olive oil. Season well. Spread on a baking sheet and roast for 30 minutes, or until tender. Wilt the spinach in 15g of the butter over a medium heat in a large pan. When no water remains, season and set aside to cool, then roughly chop.

Combine the ricotta and Parmesan and season with plenty of nutmeg and salt and pepper. Set aside. Roll the pasta out to form a rectangle 40 x 30cm, using a small amount of flour to prevent it sticking. Trim the edges so they are straight and true and lay this rectangle on a clean, flat tea towel. Wring out any water from the spinach and scatter over the pasta, leaving a border. Dot the spinach with the ricotta and scatter with roast pumpkin. Roll up from a long edge to form a sausage shape, then roll the tea towel firmly around it and tie the ends like a cracker. Bind with a couple of pieces of string. Lower the rotolo into a large pan of generously salted boiling water and poach gently for 20 minutes. Remove the rotolo from the pan and shake off excess water. Cut the strings.

Heat the remaining 2 tablespoons olive oil in a pan and add the rest of the sage leaves. Cook until crisp, then drain on absorbent kitchen paper. Melt the remaining butter in the pan and when it starts to turn golden, remove from the heat. Unwrap the rotolo, trim the ends and slice into 12 pieces. Divide between 6 warmed plates, add a few roast tomatoes and spoon the butter over. Finish with crisp sage leaves.

Special

Francesco Mazzei is immensely proud of his Calabrian roots and it shines through in his bold but refined cooking. The menu at L'Anima, his sleek London restaurant, interprets southern Italian and Moorish dishes, using as much seasonal, local produce as possible. The leafy herb, borage, grows wild across the Mediterranean and its mild, cucumber-like flavour makes a beautiful pasta filling.

Francesco Mazzei's

Borage tortelli with sage butter

SERVES 6
PREP TIME: 1 HOUR 10 MINUTES
PLUS RESTING TIME
COOKING TIME: 15 MINUTES

1 quantity rich pasta dough
(see page 251)

FOR THE PASTA FILLING:

2 shallots, finely chopped

60g butter

700g young borage greens

freshly grated nutmeg, to taste

200g best-quality ricotta, drained

50g Parmesan, finely grated,
plus extra to serve

2 teaspoons finely chopped
marjoram leaves

FOR THE SAGE BUTTER:

100g butter

about 20 small sage leaves

First make your rich pasta dough, and leave it to rest as instructed. You will need to roll it out after you have made your filling.

Gently sweat the shallots in half the butter over a low heat until softened but not coloured. Blanch the borage in salted, boiling water for a minute or so, drain, and refresh under cold water. Drain well, then chop finely and add to the shallots with a good grating of nutmeg. Stir over the heat for a few minutes, then set aside to cool.

Stir the ricotta, Parmesan, marjoram, salt and pepper into the borage. Melt the remaining butter and add to the mixture, then set aside to rest and cool while you roll out the pasta as instructed on page 251. Cut the pasta into 8cm squares with a sharp knife. Drop a teaspoon of the borage filling just off-centre in each square and brush the edges with water. Fold the dough over to create a triangle, pressing out any air as you go. Holding the triangle with the point at the top, fold the two bottom 'corners' together around your index finger and pinch together firmly to seal, using a little water if needed. Transfer to a sheet of non-stick baking paper to dry a little. Repeat. Drop the tortelli into a large saucepan of salted, simmering water and cook for 4 minutes or until they rise to the surface. Carefully remove with a slotted spoon.

Meanwhile, heat the butter and sage in a small frying pan until the butter foams and begins to turn a slightly darker brown and the leaves fizz. It should smell nutty, not burnt. The sage leaves should be crisp. Serve the drained tortelli in warmed bowls with the sage butter spooned on top, and grate a little Parmesan over to finish.

Special

Do buy these golden mushrooms whenever you see them because they are such treasures. Here, they are fried in butter with cherries and wine, and spooned over truffle-spiked pommes purée with a few truffle pearls to finish. Truffle pearls are an ingenious vegetarian version of 'caviar' made with black truffle and seaweed.

Pan-fried girolles and sour cherries

SERVES 4 AS A MAIN COURSE
PREPARATION TIME: 25 MINUTES
COOKING TIME: 35–40 MINUTES

FOR THE POMMES PURÉE:

900g floury potatoes, cut into large chunks

50g truffle butter or 50g butter and 2 teaspoons truffle oil

100ml double cream

FOR THE GIROLLES:

30g butter

1 tablespoon olive oil

2 garlic cloves, crushed

600g girolles or golden chanterelles, brushed free of dirt

1 small glass Madeira or dry sherry

100g dried sour cherries

1 small glass vegetable stock (see page 236) or quality bought stock

1 tablespoon finely chopped flat leaf parsley

4 teaspoons truffle pearls, to serve (optional)

Start with the potatoes. Steam them over simmering water for 20–25 minutes until completely tender but not falling apart. Pour all the water out of the saucepan and tip the potatoes into it. Place over a low heat for a few minutes, shaking the pan to dry them out.

Press the potatoes through a ricer if you have one – it will produce the smoothest mash – or use a masher to crush them until smooth. Beat in the truffle butter (or butter and truffle oil) and cream and season generously with salt and pepper. Keep warm.

While the potatoes steam, cook the mushrooms. Melt the butter and oil together in a large frying pan over a medium-high heat. Add the garlic and stir, followed by the mushrooms. Toss the pan now and then for a couple of minutes to brown the mushrooms all over. Remove to a plate with a slotted spoon. Pour the Madeira or sherry into the pan and reduce briskly for a minute, then add the cherries and stock and continue to simmer 5 minutes more. Return the mushrooms to the pan. Stir in the parsley and season to taste with salt and pepper.

Serve over the potato purée with a few truffle pearls (if using).

Special

Tom Pemberton, former head chef at St John in London, opened his own restaurant, Hereford Road, in Notting Hill in 2007. He fiercely champions British ingredients such as the Childwickbury goat's cheese used here: its fresh and mild flavour shines through in this comforting dish. Wild garlic and morels – spring ingredients – can be replaced with baby spinach and chanterelles in the autumn.

Tom Pemberton's

Pearl barley, mushroom and butternut squash

SERVES 4–6
PREPARATION TIME: 25 MINUTES
COOKING TIME: 1 HOUR

20g dried wild mushrooms

8 flat field mushrooms

1 small butternut squash or pumpkin, halved, deseeded and sliced

3 tablespoons olive oil

3 rosemary sprigs

3 thyme sprigs

2 shallots, finely chopped

15g butter, for sautéeing

200g pearl barley

2 tarragon stalks, roughly chopped

2 bay leaves

40g butter, softened

1 garlic clove, crushed

a small handful of fresh morels

a handful of wild garlic leaves

a squeeze of lemon

200g Childwickbury cheese, or other fresh goat's cheese

Soak the dried mushrooms in 200ml just-boiled water for 10 minutes. Only the soaking water will be needed in this dish.

Preheat the oven to 200°C (400°F/Gas 6). Place the field mushrooms and squash or pumpkin in separate trays, drizzle with olive oil, season and scatter with rosemary and thyme. Roast the mushrooms for 20 minutes and the squash or pumpkin for about 35 minutes.

Gently sauté the shallots in the butter. Rinse the pearl barley in a sieve. Add the rinsed pearl barley, tarragon stalks and bay leaves, the water from the soaked mushrooms and enough extra water to cover the grains by 2cm. Simmer for 25 minutes until the barley is just tender.

Mix the butter with the garlic to make garlic butter. When ready to serve, brown the morels in half the garlic butter and set aside. Slice the roasted mushrooms and add to the pearl barley with the squash or pumpkin and any reserved juices from roasting the vegetables. Reheat together gently with the wild garlic leaves, remaining garlic butter and a squeeze of lemon, turning through until the leaves just wilt. Remove from the heat and stir in half the Childwickbury cheese and the morels. Serve with the remaining cheese scattered over.

Special

It's a rare recipe than can star as a starter, main or cheese course. Served as a starter or main, a peppery rocket side salad wouldn't go amiss. As a dessert or cheese course, the tart will stand alone or accompanied by a little crème fraîche. Figs and hard goat's cheese also work extremely well instead of the pears and Parmesan.

Pear and Parmesan tarte tatin with thyme pastry

SERVES 6–8
PREPARATION TIME: 20 MINUTES
PLUS CHILLING TIME
COOKING TIME: 40 MINUTES

FOR THE PASTRY:

100g butter

200g plain flour, plus extra for dusting

100g Parmesan, finely grated

1 egg, beaten

1 tablespoon thyme leaves

FOR THE REST:

75g light brown sugar

50g butter

3 tablespoons balsamic vinegar

2 tablespoons chopped walnuts

1 tablespoon thyme leaves

6 ripe but firm pears, quartered and cored

Start with the pastry. Whizz the butter and flour in a food processor until it resembles fine crumbs. Add a pinch of salt and the cheese and blend for a few seconds. Then add the egg and thyme and blitz again until the pastry just comes together into a ball. Knead briefly until smooth, shape into a disc and wrap in clingfilm. Chill for at least 20 minutes.

Preheat the oven to 180°C (350°F/Gas 4). In a 25cm tatin dish or ovenproof frying pan, heat the sugar until melts, shaking and swirling from time to time so it melts evenly. Increase the heat slightly and add the butter and vinegar, allowing the mixture to bubble for a minute or so. Remove from the heat and sprinkle with the walnuts and thyme. Arrange the pears on top, peeled side down, in a snug, concentric circle.

On a lightly floured surface, roll the rested pastry into a circle 2cm larger than your dish or frying pan. Using a rolling pin to pick the pastry up, cover the fruit snugly with it like a blanket, tucking the edges in and under a little to enclose everything securely. Bake for 30 minutes until the pastry is golden and the caramel is bubbling up at the edges. Leave to cool for 10 minutes before placing an inverted plate (ideally one with a lip to catch the sauce) on top of the pan. Wearing oven gloves and holding the plate and pan tightly, flip the whole lot over so that the plate is underneath and the pan is upside down on top of it. Remove the pan to reveal the tart, pushing any dislodged pears back into place if necessary.

Special

This is a decadently rich soufflé cake that will fall and sink slowly as it cools. The middle is dense and mousse-like, the edges crisp and the salted caramel ribbon swirling through the chocolate gives it an edge over any other torte. It's a good idea to make it a few hours in advance, and serve when cool but not chilled.

Bitter chocolate and salted caramel torte

SERVES 12
PREPARATION TIME: 30 MINUTES
COOKING TIME: ABOUT 40 MINUTES

FOR THE SALTED CARAMEL:

175g golden caster sugar

120ml double cream

½ teaspoon sea salt flakes

120g unsalted butter, cubed

FOR THE TORTE:

250g dark chocolate (at least 70% cocoa solids), in pieces

160g unsalted butter, cubed

175g golden caster sugar

1 teaspoon vanilla extract

120g ground almonds

5 medium egg yolks

6 medium egg whites

Line a 25cm springform cake tin with non-stick baking paper. To make the salted caramel, pour the sugar into a heavy-based pan and add 3 tablespoons of water. Heat gently, stirring only until the sugar dissolves. Turn the heat up to medium-high and allow the syrup to come to the boil undisturbed. Simmer briskly and watch like a hawk until the caramel turns a rich amber colour. Swirl the pan to prevent 'hot spots' but don't stir or the caramel will crystallise. Remove the pan from the heat and stir in the cream and salt; it's sure to hiss and splutter. Now stir in the butter cubes until a smooth caramel forms and set aside to cool.

Preheat the oven to 180°C (350°F/Gas 4). To make the torte, melt the chocolate, butter and sugar together in a heatproof bowl set over simmering water. (You can melt everything in a saucepan set over a very low heat if you prefer, but go gently in case it burns.) Remove from the heat and stir until smooth, then mix in the vanilla and almonds, followed by the egg yolks, one by one.

Whisk the egg whites in a clean bowl until they hold stiff peaks. Using a metal spoon, fold 1 large tablespoon of the egg whites into the chocolate mixture to loosen it, then fold in the rest, being careful to retain as much air as possible. Scrape into the tin and smooth the top. Pour or spoon the caramel over the top in a big circular swirl, moving from the centre out. Use a skewer or sharp knife to mix the caramel a little deeper into the batter but don't overdo it. Bake for about 30 minutes until puffed up but still wobbly in the centre. Cool completely in the tin before slicing and serving with cream or ice cream.

Special

If an almond tart isn't deep and buttery with a burnished shell, it isn't worth the effort or the calories. There will be no disappointments here with this divine tart, which delivers on every count.

Rich almond tart with red berry compote

SERVES 10–12
PREPARATION TIME: 40 MINUTES
PLUS CHILLING TIME
COOKING TIME: 1 HOUR 20 MINUTES

FOR THE PASTRY:

225g plain flour, plus a little extra for dusting

125g butter, diced

½ teaspoon salt

60g icing sugar

1 egg yolk

2–4 teaspoons iced water

FOR THE ALMOND FILLING:

250g blanched almonds

2 tablespoons plain flour

250 unsalted butter

275g golden caster sugar

1 vanilla pod, split and seeds scraped out

4 eggs

300g seasonal berries, such as blueberries, raspberries, blackberries, redcurrants or blackcurrants

FOR THE COMPOTE:

300g seasonal berries, as above

3 tablespoons golden caster sugar

1 tablespoon balsamic vinegar

chilled crème fraîche, to serve

Preheat the oven to 170°C (325°F/Gas 3). To make the pastry, pulse the flour, butter, salt and sugar in a food processor until the mixture looks like fine breadcrumbs. Add the egg yolk and 2 teaspoons of the iced water then pulse just enough to bring it all together into a dough. You may need another teaspoon or 2 of iced water but don't add too much or the pastry will go claggy. Knead very briefly until smooth, form into a disc and wrap in clingfilm. Chill for at least 30 minutes. Roll out the pastry on a lightly floured surface until it forms a large enough circle to line a deep 25cm tart tin that has a removable base. You shouldn't need to butter the tin first. Press the pastry right into the tin and use a sharp knife to trim off any overhanging excess. Chill for at least 30 minutes.

Meanwhile, use a food processor to grind the almonds and plain flour together finely. The flour should stop the almonds turning oily. Tip into a bowl. Now add to the food processor the butter, 250g sugar and vanilla seeds (save the pod) and mix until light and fluffy. Add the eggs, one by one, with the motor still running, until completely blended. Scrape into the bowl with the almonds and mix well. Scatter the berries across the base of the tart case and spoon the almond filling over the fruit. Smooth the top and sprinkle evenly with the remaining sugar. Bake for about 1 hour 20 minutes or so until golden and risen.

Meanwhile, make the compote. Gently heat the berries with the empty vanilla pod, sugar and vinegar until the fruit just starts to bleed its juice. Remove from the heat. Cool the tart before serving with the berry compote and crème fraîche.

Special

I find it much more effective to make smaller quantities of really special conserves than endless pots of everyday jams that sit sullenly at the back of the cupboard for months. This black fig jam is intensely rich and it's the perfect foil for cheeses, crisp crackers or perhaps with little blue cheese tarts still warm from the oven.

Black fig jam for cheese and canapés

MAKES 2 JARS
PREPARATION TIME: 5 MINUTES
PLUS MACERATING TIME
COOKING TIME: 40 MINUTES

800g ripe black figs, halved

½ teaspoon fennel seeds

300g golden caster sugar

juice of 1 lemon

Stir the figs, fennel seeds and sugar together in a bowl. Cover and set aside for 4 hours or chill overnight.

Tip the fig mixture into a large saucepan and slowly heat through. Once the mixture has come to the boil, scoop out the figs with a slotted spoon and reserve in a bowl. Turn up the heat and simmer the syrup briskly until it reaches the 'hard ball stage' at around 120°C (235°F/Gas ½). If you don't have a thermometer, scoop a tiny amount of syrup out with a teaspoon and drop into a cup of cold water; it should form a hard ball if ready.

Return the figs to the syrup and continue to simmer for about 25 minutes until thickened, stirring occasionally to break the fruit up. Stir in the lemon juice.

Pot in sterilised jars and keep in a cool, dark place.

Special

Basics

Chapter Nine

These delicious butters are more suggestions than rigid recipes, and have many variations. Group complimentary ingredients together and experiment, but start with the ideas below. The butters can be tossed with simple steamed vegetables, cooked pasta, wholegrains and more. You can even freeze them so you have them on standby.

Flavoured butters

MAKES 250G PER IDEA
PREPARATION TIME: 15 MINUTES
PLUS CHILLING TIME

flavourings (see method)

250g unsalted butter, softened

1 teaspoon sea salt

Beat your choice of flavourings below into the softened butter with the salt. Spoon onto a sheet of greaseproof paper and roll into a cylinder, twisting the ends like a cracker. Chill for at least an hour to firm up so that you can slice circles off when needed. The wrapped and chilled butters will keep for at least 4 weeks. If you choose to freeze the butter, slice into discs before wrapping the cylinder. Keep the frozen butter for up to 3 months, snapping off a disc or 2 as needed.

Lime and chilli butter

Finely grated zest of 2 limes; 2 red chillies, deseeded and finely chopped.

Blue cheese and black pepper butter

75g Roquefort, finely crumbled; 1 teaspoon thyme leaves; 2 teaspoons crushed black peppercorns.

Garlic-herb butter

2 fat garlic cloves, crushed; 3 tablespoons finely chopped basil leaves or chives; 2 tablespoons pine nuts, toasted and chopped.

Parsley butter

3 tablespoons finely chopped parsley; ½ garlic clove, crushed; ½ teaspoon crushed black peppercorns.

Mayonnaise

2 egg yolks
1 teaspoon Dijon mustard
275ml very mild olive oil
a good squeeze of lemon

Blend or beat the egg yolks with a generous seasoning of salt and pepper and the mustard. As you blend or beat, start to add the olive oil, drop by slow drop. Tentatively increase the drops to a thin trickle as you continue to blend. Add about half the oil then beat in the lemon juice. Continue adding the oil as before until it has all gone and the mayonnaise is thick and glossy. Taste and add a touch more salt, pepper or lemon juice if needed. To make herb mayonnaise stir in 2 tablespoons chopped fresh herbs at the end. To make aïoli add 2–3 fat, crushed garlic cloves with the egg yolks. To make red pepper aïoli stir 2 roughly-puréed roasted red peppers (from a jar is fine) into the finished aïoli. Makes 1 cup.

Gomashio

3 tablespoons sea salt
400g sesame seeds

Toast the salt in a dry frying pan, stirring often, until it turns grey. Tip into a pestle and mortar, spice grinder or food processor. Toast the sesame seeds in the same pan until they smell fragrant. Grind the salt and seeds together, by hand or by machine, until broken down but not too smooth or the mixture will become oily. Store in a tightly sealed jar and use within 2 months. Makes 1 large jar.

Balsamic vinaigrette

2 tablespoons balsamic vinegar
a pinch of caster sugar
4 tablespoons extra virgin olive oil
1 teaspoon Dijon mustard
1 tablespoon chopped basil

This dressing is especially good with tomatoes and roast Mediterranean vegetables. For variation, you could also add a whisper of garlic before blending. Place all the ingredients in a mini food processor with 1 tablespoon water and pulse until blended. Makes about 120ml.

Vegetable stock

1 tablespoon sunflower oil
2 large onions, sliced
2 large carrots, sliced
10 celery sticks, sliced
6 garlic cloves, bruised
4 chard stalks, sliced
60g brown lentils
3 bay leaves
a small bunch of parsley stalks
1 teaspoon black peppercorns
1 teaspoon sea salt

Heat the oil in a large saucepan. Slowly brown the onions and carrots, stirring, for about 20 minutes. The vegetables should be golden and caramelised. Add the remaining ingredients with 2 litres cold water, bring to a simmer and bubble gently for 1 hour. Strain and discard the vegetables. Return the stock to the pan on the heat and reduce to the desired strength. Makes about 1.8 litres.

Horseradish dressing

2 tablespoons crème fraîche
4 tablespoons walnut oil
1 tablespoon finely grated horseradish,
or more to taste
juice of 1 lemon
a pinch of caster sugar

This is strictly for robustly flavoured
vegetables and leaves, as it takes a certain
strength to stand up to peppery horseradish.
Whisk all the ingredients together with
2 tablespoons cold water to loosen. Season
to taste with salt and pepper. Makes 120ml.

Salsa verde dressing

1 small bunch parsley, chopped
½ small bunch mint, chopped
75ml extra virgin olive oil, plus extra if needed
1 fat garlic clove, crushed
2 tablespoons capers, rinsed, drained and chopped
1½ tablespoons Dijon mustard
2 tablespoons red wine vinegar

In a small bowl, cover the chopped herbs
with olive oil – start with 75ml and see how you
go. Stir in the remaining ingredients and season
with salt and pepper to taste. The sauce should
have a spoonable consistency so add more
olive oil if needed. Makes about 200ml.

Pesto

1 fat garlic clove, roughly chopped
a pinch of sea salt
a large handful of basil leaves
60g pine nuts
about 100ml extra virgin olive oil
70g Parmesan, finely grated

In a food processor pulse together the garlic,
salt, basil leaves and pine nuts, scraping down
the sides now and then. Add the cheese and
trickle in the oil until blended. To make parsley,
peppery rocket or watercress pesto, replace
the basil with your herb of choice and swap
the pine nuts with roughly chopped, blanched
almonds. To make sun-dried tomato pesto,
simply add 5 drained and chopped sun-dried
tomato halves when pounding or blending the
basil. To make vegan pesto, omit the cheese
and increase the quantity of pine nuts or
almonds to 3 tablespoons. Makes 1 jar.

Sweet lemon dressing

½ garlic clove, crushed
1 tablespoon mild honey
1 teaspoon wholegrain mustard
finely grated zest and juice of 1 lemon
90ml olive oil

Robust leaves – chicory, radicchio, rocket
and watercress – all bring out the best in
this dressing. If you'd rather use a milder leaf
you might want to replace the honey with
2 tablespoons finely grated Parmesan to pep
it up and balance out the flavours. Combine all
the ingredients in a screw-top jar with salt and
pepper, and shake until thoroughly blended.
Makes about 100ml.

Sauces

Fig tapenade

Place 100g ready-to-eat, chopped dried figs in a pan with 100ml water and simmer for 15 minutes, stirring, until tender. Remove from the heat and cool. Use a pestle and mortar or food processor to crush ½ garlic clove, 150g stoned Kalamata olives, 2 tablespoons rinsed and drained capers, the figs and their liquid, a twist of black pepper and 2 tablespoons thyme leaves. Pulse and loosen with extra virgin olive oil.

Blender hollandaise

Melt 120g butter in a small pan. Whizz 2 egg yolks in a small blender with 2 tablespoons boiling water and season with a pinch of salt and a little black pepper. With the motor on, very gradually trickle in the hot butter until a thick sauce forms. Add a couple of tablespoons of lemon juice and blend again. Check the lemon and seasoning before serving.

Gorgonzola

Soften 2 finely chopped shallots in a little butter until translucent. Add 150g chopped Gorgonzola (or Roquefort if you prefer) and stir gently until the cheese melts. Stir in 100ml of double cream and mix well. Season with black pepper. A little finely chopped parsley stirred in at the end makes a nice addition. Delicious stirred through pasta.

4

Walnut tarator

This Turkish sauce is a bit like a nut pesto. It is wonderful with roast or grilled vegetables or in flatbread wraps. Pulse 200g shelled walnuts in a food processor with a fat, crushed garlic clove and a good pinch of salt until quite finely ground. Gradually pour in 2 tablespoons red wine vinegar, 100ml water and 60ml extra virgin olive oil as you process again to form a creamy but not completely smooth sauce.

6

Best tomato

Peel and halve a small onion and lightly bash a whole, peeled garlic clove. Place in a saucepan with 2 x 400g tins of best quality plum tomatoes and 75g butter (or 75ml extra virgin olive oil if you prefer). Place over a very gentle heat and slowly simmer, stirring occasionally, for about 40–50 minutes. Season with salt and pepper and discard the onion before using. The garlic will have melted away.

5

Béchamel

In a saucepan bring to the boil: 1 litre whole milk; 1 small, peeled and halved onion; 10 black peppercorns; and 2 bay leaves. Remove from the heat and infuse for 20 minutes or so. Melt 60g butter in a pan and add 60g plain flour, stirring until a smooth paste forms. Cook gently for a minute or so, stirring, then gradually add the infused milk, tentatively at first, beating all the while. Use a whisk at this stage to prevent lumps. When the milk has been incorporated, bring the sauce to the boil and simmer gently for a couple of minutes. Season and add a generous grating of nutmeg. Cover to prevent a skin forming and set aside to cool.

Chilli tomato jam

10 mild red chillies, deseeded
2 shallots, roughly chopped
4cm piece ginger, roughly chopped
2 lemongrass stalks, roughly chopped
200g cherry tomatoes, halved
75g palm sugar or light brown sugar
4 tablespoons rice wine vinegar
2 tablespoons soy sauce

Place the chillies in a food processor with
the shallots, ginger and lemongrass. Pulse,
scraping down the sides every few seconds,
until finely chopped. Scrape into a saucepan
with the tomatoes and sugar, and cook over a
medium-high heat for about 20 minutes. Stir
often until the liquid evaporates and the sugar
caramelises. Now add the vinegar and soy
sauce and simmer until the liquid evaporates.
Season with salt to taste. Spoon into a
sterilised jar, cover and keep chilled for up
to 4 weeks. Makes 1 large jar.

Rustic, slow-roast tomato sauce

300g slow-roast tomatoes (see recipe this page)
500g jar passata
a small handful of basil leaves
2 tablespoons extra virgin olive oil

This is a deep and intense sauce that can be
made almost instantly if you have a batch of
slow-roast tomatoes to hand. Add chopped red
chilli or crushed garlic before blending to ring
the changes. Simply blend all the ingredients
together in a food processor or blender until
almost smooth. Makes about 720g.

Slow-roast tomatoes

1kg ripe, sweet tomatoes, halved
2 tablespoons caster sugar
2 tablespoons chopped fresh rosemary leaves
3 garlic cloves, finely chopped

Preheat the oven to 110ºC (225ºF/Gas ½).
Lay the tomatoes out on 2 baking sheets, cut
sides up. Sprinkle with salt and pepper, sugar,
rosemary and garlic, and drizzle with olive oil.
Roast for about 4 hours – depending on the
size or variety of tomato – until shrunken and a
little blackened at the edges. If your tomatoes
are very large they can take up to 6 hours but
if you use cherry tomatoes, they will take
about 3 hours.

Pepper compote

3 red peppers
3 long red chillies
1 red onion, halved and finely sliced
2 tablespoons olive oil
1 garlic clove, crushed
1 tablespoon light brown sugar
3 tablespoons sherry vinegar
a pinch of sweet smoked paprika

Blacken the peppers and chillies over a gas
flame or under a very hot grill, turning with
tongs every minute or so until charred all over.
Remove to a bowl, cover with clingfilm and set
aside for a few minutes. Scrape the skin from
peppers and chillies, halve them and scrape out
the seeds. Chop the flesh roughly. Gently fry
the onion in the oil until softened, then reduce
the heat and add the garlic and chopped
peppers. Cook for 5 minutes more, add the
sugar, vinegar and paprika and cook until
caramelised. Spoon into a sterilised jar or dish
and keep chilled. Makes 1 jar.

  *Basics*

Satay sauce

1 garlic clove, chopped
2 shallots, roughly chopped
1–2 red chillies, roughly chopped
1 tablespoon groundnut oil
2 teaspoons caster sugar
150g peanuts, toasted and roughly chopped
1 tablespoon soy sauce
400ml coconut milk
juice of 1 lime

Gently fry the garlic, shallots and red chillies in the oil until soft but not coloured. Add the sugar and peanuts and cook for a further 2 minutes until caramelised. Now stir in the soy and coconut milk and simmer for 5 minutes. Keep the texture chunky, or blend briefly in a food processor. Add the lime juice and season with a little extra soy if needed. Satay sauce will keep in the refrigerator for 2 weeks or more. Makes about 500ml.

Charmoula dressing

1 small bunch coriander
1 small bunch parsley
1 tablespoon cumin seeds, toasted
finely grated zest and juice of 1 lemon
75ml extra virgin olive oil
½ teaspoon salt
1 garlic clove, crushed
½ teaspoon paprika
1 teaspoon ras el hanout

Place all the ingredients in a food processor and pulse until finely chopped. Add a little more olive oil if it seems too thick and season with black pepper. Keep covered in the refrigerator for up to 2 weeks, ready to use whenever the mood takes you. Makes 1 jar.

Ginger and lime dipping sauce

60ml boiling water
1½ tablespoons caster sugar
2 tablespoons vegetarian fish sauce or soy sauce
2 tablespoons rice wine vinegar
juice of ½ lime
4cm piece ginger, finely chopped
1 fat garlic clove, finely chopped
1 red chilli, deseeded and finely chopped (optional)

Pour the boiling water over the sugar and stir to dissolve. Add all the remaining ingredients – leaving out the chilli if you like – and mix well. Leave to stand for a few minutes before using. Makes 100ml.

Pickled fruit for cheese and salads

500ml red wine vinegar
2 tablespoons caster sugar
1 tablespoon sea salt
1 tablespoon black peppercorns
3 rosemary sprigs
500g fresh fruit, trimmed, stoned, sliced or halved, as appropriate

Place all the ingredients except the fruit in a large saucepan, add 150ml water and bring to the boil. Add the fruit. Divide between sterilised jars and seal. Keep in a cool, dark place for at least 2 weeks before opening – a month if you can. To serve, simply remove as much fruit as you need from the jar with a slotted spoon. The leftover pickling liquid can be strained and used in salad dressings. Once opened, the pickles will last for at least 4 weeks, but keep refrigerated. Makes 3 jars.

Menu Ideas

Winter dinner

Blood orange, mozzarella, toasted
sourdough and radicchio salad (page 82)

Parsnip, sage and
mascarpone risotto (page 172)

Rich almond tart with
red berry compote (page 228)

Black fig jam, with cheese
and crackers (page 230)

Spring brunch

Mango and cashew smoothies (page 32)

Toasted honey and pumpkin seed
granola with yoghurt, served
with rhubarb compote (page 34)

Baked ricotta with avocado (page 24)

Pizza Bianca (page 136)

Salad potato griddle cakes with olives
and poached eggs (page 160)

Sunday lunch

Butter bean and celeriac velouté
with charmoula (page 126)

Pearl barley, mushroom and
butternut squash (page 222)

Greens dressed with
walnut tarator (page 186)

Pear and Parmesan tarte tatin
with thyme pastry (page 224)

Fast dinner
for friends

Shopska salad (page 168)

Fennel and lemon risotto (page 201)

Asparagus with brioche crumbs (page 186)

Warm salted caramel sauce with quality
bought vanilla ice cream
(make the salted caramel from the bitter chocolate
and salted caramel torte recipe on page 226)

Menu Ideas

Romantic dinner

White gazpacho (page 116)

Pumpkin and spinach rotolo with
sage butter (as a main course, page 216)

Bitter chocolate and
salted caramel torte (page 226)

Pickled fruit to serve with a
cheese platter (page 244)

Southeast Asian lunch

Summer spring rolls (page 206)

Crispy five-spice tofu with
soy dipping sauce (page 154)

Braised baby aubergines with bok choy,
peanuts and Thai basil, served with
steamed rice (page 182)

Ripe melon, papaya and
mango slices, to finish

Summer picnic

Gazpacho Andaluz (page 114)

Pissaladière (page 194)

Nectarine and tomato salad with buffalo
mozzarella (page 210)

No-knead sourdough loaf (page 134)

Summer berries with home-made yoghurt
(instructions for yoghurt page 36)

Drinks party

Roast, spiced chickpeas (page 105)

Robust caponata spooned
onto panelle (page 46)

Betel leaf wraps with coconut
and cashews (page 208)

Puy lentil hummus, carrot and cumin
hummus, garlic toasts (page 54)

Chervil pancakes with aubergine caviar
and pomegranate (page 204)

Glossary

Betel leaves
The edible leaves of the Piper betle plant are used extensively throughout Southeast Asia. When used as a wrap for food, keep the glossy side of each heart-shaped leaf on the outside. Look for them in the chilled fresh vegetable section of Southeast Asian food shops. Keep refrigerated and use within a few days of purchase.

Blind baking
Pastry tart shells often need to be cooked before filling to ensure they are crisp and not soggy underneath. To do this, line a tart tin with raw pastry and chill. Cover with non-stick baking paper or foil and heap baking beans, dried pulses or uncooked rice into the tart cavity, then bake at 190°C (375°F/Gas 5) for 15 minutes. Remove the beans and foil or paper, and return the tart to the oven for a further 5–10 minutes until the pastry looks dry and 'sandy' but still pale.

Burrata
This decadently rich, fresh buffalo or cow's cheese from southern Italy is similar to mozzarella, but each sphere of cheese contains an indulgent centre of cream. The trick is to eat it as fresh as possible to enjoy the best of its mild, buttery flavour. You can order it from good Italian delis.

Buttermilk
Traditionally, buttermilk was a watery by-product of butter making, but these days is made by souring skimmed milk to produce a dairy product similar to thin yoghurt. Buttermilk produces tender pancakes and light, quick breads when combined with bicarbonate of soda.

Chinese black vinegar
This sweetly complex vinegar is made from glutinous rice and malt. Use in small amounts in dipping sauces, marinades, stir-fries and braises. Rice vinegar with a pinch of brown sugar added is a good alternative.

Chipotle pepper
Jalepeno peppers are smoke-dried in Mexico to make the fiery and complex chipotle. They are available dried, or in a paste in jars, and will add smoky heat to your cooking. Add a whole pepper to simmering stews or soups, or a teaspoonful or two of the paste. Go carefully as the heat is intense.

Daikon, mooli or white radish
This large, carrot-shaped radish is crisp, white and very popular throughout Asia. Because of its size and mild flavour, it is often sliced or shredded and then pickled, then eaten as a condiment or in stir-fries. You'll find them in speciality food shops or large supermarkets. Store in the fridge or a cool larder.

Dry roasting and oven toasting
Spices, nuts and seeds often benefit from being gently toasted in a completely dry frying pan over a medium heat, before grinding or using in a recipe. This will bring out the fragrance and make nuts taste nuttier by coaxing out their oils. To toast nuts and seeds in the oven, spread out on a baking tray and bake at 150°C (300°F/Gas 2) for 8–10 minutes (keep an eye on them!), shaking the tin once or twice to redistribute to ensure they toast evenly.

Gram flour
Also known as chickpea or besan flour, gram flour is made from chickpeas. Gluten-free, it has a toasty, slightly nutty taste and is fantastic in batters and can hold vegetables together in bhajis or pakoras. It is famously used in socca, the traditional Niçoise fritters, and the similar Italian farinata and panelle.

Harissa
Based on red chillies, tomatoes and hot paprika, this oily North African paste often contains other spices and aromatics like cumin, coriander, garlic, lemons, peppers and even rosebuds. Buy from speciality shops or supermarkets and refrigerate once opened. Add to marinades and dressings, tagines, soups and dips.

Lemongrass
To use this mellow, lemony grass in curry pastes, dressings, stir-fries and sauces, trim the hard base from the roots, snip about 3cm off the top, then peel away the outer layers to reveal the softer, purplish core. Chop this soft middle into rings or fine dice, discarding any hard stalk. Bash the stalk with a rolling pin and add to rice, or to sauces as they simmer. Lemongrass combines successfully with sugar in sweet dishes.

Pomegranate molasses
This sweet and sour, dark red syrup is made by boiling pomegranate juice down until it is thick and sticky. Its tart flavour is used in many Middle Eastern dishes, most commonly to enhance meat and poultry, but is also wonderful added to dressings for roast vegetables. Lemon juice mixed with honey, or tamarind, can be used as a substitute. It can also be diluted to make a drink.

Pomelo
This large, green or yellow citrus fruit is native to Southeast Asia. Its pale yellow or pink flesh (depending on the variety) will separate easily into segments if you prise away the thick layer of white pith and membranes. To do this, score the fruit into sections from top to bottom and peel away the skin and as much white pith as possible, then pull the fruit in half.

Ras el hanout
Ras el hanout translates literally as 'top of the shop' in Arabic; it's a fragrant Moroccan spice mix blended from the best of the spice merchant's shop. Some versions contain over one hundred different ingredients, but it commonly includes coriander, cumin, cinnamon, turmeric, clove, nutmeg, cardamom and chilli. Use in marinades, dressings and sauces.

Rice wine vinegar
This vinegar made from fermented rice is commonly used in Southeast Asian cooking and is pale, clear and sharp – ideal for dipping sauces, pickles and marinades. It is widely available in supermarkets and speciality food shops.

Rich pasta dough

Make this delicious pasta dough for Francesco Mazzei's borage tortelli with sage butter recipe on page 218, or your own pasta dishes.

INGREDIENTS

300g type 00 flour, or as needed
9 egg yolks
semolina flour, for dusting

Pour the flour onto a clean work surface and make a well in the centre like a volcano crater. Tip the egg yolks into the centre. Using one hand, mix the yolks into the flour gradually, using a circular motion to incorporate more and more flour as you go. Stop when enough flour has been mixed in to make a slightly 'flaky' ball. You may not need all the flour, or you may need a little more. Wash and dry your hands, then knead the dough for about 10 minutes until very smooth and silken. Add extra flour as needed to stop it sticking. Wrap in clingfilm and leave to rest for at least 30 minutes or up to 1 hour. You can make the dough a day ahead and chill, well wrapped.

When you have made the filling, cut the dough into 6 even pieces (cover the unused dough to stop it drying out). Run each piece through a pasta machine on its widest setting. Do this several times, folding the dough over on itself twice before you pass it through the machine again. Dust with semolina to stop it sticking. Don't be alarmed if the dough looks a bit 'lacy' at one point – it will work out in the end if you fold it and pass it through the machine a few more times. Now, stop folding the pasta over and just pass it through the rollers, reducing the setting one notch each time. When you reach the thinnest setting but one, lay the rolled sheet of dough out on a work surface dusted with semolina. If you don't own a pasta machine, roll the pasta out by hand on a lightly floured surface, until very thin. Continue with the borage tortelli and sage butter recipe as instructed, or whatever recipe you are are using.

Sambal oelek

This vibrant Indonesian chilli paste is used to pep up curries, marinades and dipping sauces. Add it sparingly because its red chilli content can pack quite a punch. Substitute with finely chopped red chilli, ground with a little salt, if you can't find it.

Seasoning

The finest sea salt flakes and freshly crushed black peppercorns really will make a difference to your cooking, and you will probably need to add less than if you use generic table salt and sneeze-worthy pre-ground pepper. Keep tasting your food and adjusting the seasoning accordingly. If you add a touch too much salt by mistake, a squeeze of lemon juice or a spoonful of vinegar can remedy the situation.

Soy sauce

This thin, salty Southeast Asian sauce is made from fermented soy beans, wheat, yeast, salt and sugar. It is available in light or dark: dark soy is slightly thicker and sweeter than light. If you are avoiding wheat, seek out the wheat-free equivalent, tamari.

Sterilising

To sterilise bottles, jars and lids for preserves and pickles, wash in hot, soapy water then carefully rinse again with hot water from the kettle. Preheat the oven to 150°C (300°F/Gas 2) and dry the jars, bottles and lids on a tray in the oven for 10 minutes. Fill them with the hot preserve or pickle while still warm to prevent cracking, and seal immediately by screwing the lids or stoppers on tightly.

Tahini

This sesame seed paste is used in one form or another throughout the Middle East and Asia. The variety used in this book, and most commonly found in Europe, is light tahini paste, so-called because the sesame seeds have been hulled before roasting and grinding. This process takes away much of the bitterness found in rustic versions. The putty-coloured paste should be chilled after opening. Use it make hummus, dressings and sauces.

Tamarind

The sticky seed pod from the tamarind tree is commonly used in Southeast Asian and Indian dishes to add an appealing honeyed sourness. The brown pods house hard seeds that are embedded in a dense, sweet and sour pulp. Convenient, ready-sieved tamarind purée can be purchased in jars, but the blocks of fresh tamarind pulp have a better flavour. If using a block of pulp, place 40g of it in a bowl and cover with 150ml boiling water. Leave to soften for a few minutes, then stir well and sieve to remove the fibres and seeds. Use as you would the bought purée.

Tempeh

Made from fermented or cultured soy beans, tempeh is a pressed, pale cake with a firm texture that is rich in protein, fibre and vitamins. It can be sliced, cubed or even grated to be grilled, stir-fried or added to vegetable patties or curries. Tempeh responds well to brining or marinating with aromatics and spices, and is readily available from health food shops.

Toasted sesame oil

This amber-hued oil is pressed from roasted or toasted sesame seeds. This process lends the oil a dark caramel colour and the aromatic flavour essential to many Chinese, Korean and some Southeast Asian dishes. Add a few drops at the end of cooking so the heat does not destroy the oil's flavour, and use sparingly or its nutty tones may be overwhelming.

Vegetarian 'fish' sauce

You may have to search hard for this ingredient, but it does exist! Good Southeast Asian shops should stock bottles of this salty, mushroom-based alternative to a true fish sauce. If you can't find it, substitute with light soy sauce.

Index

Index

Acknowledgements

Without the commission from, and vision of, Catie Ziller, this project would never have come to fruition. Thank you, Catie. Here's hoping it encourages everyone to cut back on the meat eating now and then.

Sue, your patience and serenity throughout the editing process have been astounding – thank you so much for all the extra words and help. Lisa, thank you for being so funny and kind day after day, and for not minding the chaos in your kitchen, in spite of which, you managed to take particularly stunning pictures! Rashna, you have worked so inspiringly to create these beautiful pages and have never failed to be utterly charming and cheerful. And lovely Lou, who was a great help on shoot days, you are simply marvellous. What would we have done without you? Alice Chadwick has added such individuality and humour through her wonderful illustrations.

A special thank you goes to Francesco for the bag of delicious goodies he sent to the shoot and to Petersham Nurseries for so kindly lending the beautiful zinc table (our 'magic' table) that brought so many of the photographs in this book to life.

To chefs Stéphane, Skye, Rowley, Francesco and Tom, thank you for so generously contributing your recipes. They have made the book even more special.

Stéphane Reynaud Villa9trois – 28, rue Colbert, 93100 Montreuil, France. Tel: +33 (0)1 48 58 17 37, www.villa9trois.com. **Skye Gyngell** Petersham Nurseries Cafe – Church Lane, Off Petersham Road, Richmond, TW10 7AG, England. Tel: +44 (0)208 605 3627, www.petershamnurseries.com. **Rowley Leigh** Le Café Anglais – 8 Porchester Gardens, London W2 4DB, England. Tel: +44 (0)20 7221 1415, www.lecafeanglais.co.uk. **Francesco Mazzei** L'Anima – 1 Snowden Street, Broadgate West, London EC2A 2DQ, England. Tel: +44 (0)207 422 7000, www.lanima.co.uk. **Tom Pemberton** Hereford Road Restaurant – 3 Hereford Road, Westbourne Grove, London W2 4AB, England. Tel: +44 (0)20 7727 1144, www.herefordroad.org

Publisher: Catie Ziller
Art Director: Rashna Mody Clark
Editor: Sue Quinn
Illustrator: Alice Chadwick
Translation: Catherine Vandevyvere

First published by Marabout (Hachette Livre) in French in 2010
This edition published in 2011 by Murdoch Books Pty Limited

Murdoch Books Australia
Pier 8/9
23 Hickson Road
Millers Point NSW 2000
Phone: +61 (0) 2 8220 2000
Fax: +61 (0) 2 8220 2558
www.murdochbooks.com.au

Murdoch Books UK Limited
Erico House, 6th Floor
93–99 Upper Richmond Road
Putney, London SW15 2TG
Phone: +44 (0) 20 8785 5995
Fax: +44 (0) 20 8785 5985
www.murdochbooks.co.uk

National Library of Australia Cataloguing-in-Publication entry
Author: Hart, Alice.
Title: Vegetarian / Alice Hart.
Edition: 1st ed.
ISBN: 978-1-74266-339-5 (pbk.)
Notes: Includes index.
Subjects: Vegetarian cooking.
Dewey Number: 641.5636

A catalogue record for this book is available from the British Library.

Printed by 1010 Printing International Limited, China.